# Papa Said

# PAPA SAID

Winona Ruth Gunther

*To my children, grandchildren, and great-grandchildren,
in memory of Papa and Mamma*

# Preface

After a visit to my birthplace in Indiana, my children and grandchildren urged me to write down memories of my childhood. I chose to insert some history so they would better understand what their ancestors went through and what a rich heritage they have.

The first five years of my life were spent on a 240-acre farm that had been handed down through the family from my great-grandfather, John Anderson, referred to as "Scotch John." Our farm was located between the Tippecanoe and Wabash rivers, approximately 20 miles northeast of their confluence near Lafayette and Battleground (once known as Prophet's Town).

Many Indian tribes roamed the Wabash Valley prior to the establishment of the Keth-tip-pe-can-nunk trading post in the eighteenth century. This post was referred to as "Tippecanoe." The village thrived until 1791, when it was razed in an attempt to scatter the Indians, opening the land to white settlers.

In May, 1808, two Shawnee brothers, Chief Tecumseh and Tenskwatawa ("The Prophet") left their native Ohio and were allowed to settle on these Potawatomi- and Kickapoo-held lands. They planned to unite many tribes into a Great Indian Confederacy, their equivalent of

Washington D.C. At one time, as many as 1000 Indians were based here.

White settlers became worried by the increasing activities and power of Tecumseh and his followers.

In late summer of 1811, Indiana Territorial Governor, William Henry Harrison, with approximately 1000 men, mostly Indiana Territorial Militia, camped out on a wooded hill above Prophet's Town. Harrison met with The Prophet and it was mutually agreed there would be no hostilities until a meeting could be held the next day. Harrison did not trust the Prophet and stationed guards all night. The Indians attacked before dawn. A bloody battle ensued, ending Tecumseh's plans. He left Indiana with his followers and joined the British to fight the United States in the War of 1812. The Prophet was stripped of his authority and wandered the state with his followers.

My great grandfather, Scotch John Anderson, emigrated from Scotland and settled near friends in Ohio. His first three sons were born there. In March of 1812, he moved to Indiana and purchased 160 acres of uncleared land. He paid the government price of $2 per acre. The land was located two miles southwest of Hanover and one mile south of the Carmel Associate Presbyterian Church, in Jefferson County, Indiana Territory. Being close to his church was most important to Scotch John. He was a member of the Associate Presbyterian congregation, known as "Seceders," because they had seceded from the United Presbyterian church. They were stern, God-fearing people, strong in their faith, and kept the Sabbath. No work or travel was done on Sunday if it could be avoided. They were strongly opposed to the practice of slavery (even before 1800), intoxication, profanity, games of chance, dancing, and secret societies. Scotch John raised his children in that faith, and they carried it on with their children. This is how I was raised.

After the Battle of Tippecanoe, the area was thought to be fairly safe, even though Indians were still quite numerous and scattered throughout the territory. This belief was shattered on September 3, 1812. While most of the men were off fighting the British, a group of Indians, thought to be mostly Shawneee and led by Missilemotaw, killed two men in the woods. They proceeded to the small settlement of Pigeon Roost, about two miles away, slaughtering one man, five women, and 16 children, wiping out whole families and burning homes. This raid was coordinated with raids on Fort Wayne and Fort Harrison.

In 1834, Scotch John again moved his family, this time into dense forests in Carroll County, Indiana. He was a shrewd investor and followed progress. He chose his farm near an Associate Presbyterian Congregation. He cleared his land and built a home. This is the land on which I was born.

Scotch John's son, John Brookie Anderson (my grandfather), was 52 when he married Agnes Eliza Alderdice, a spinster school teacher several years younger than he. Agnes was the daughter of Reverend Thomas Hance Alderdice, a Presbyterian minister, and Izabella Smith Anderson. The ceremony was performed by Reverend Alderdice in April of 1881.

Grandpa and Grandma Alderdice and family

Rev. Thomas Hance Alderdice

Grandpa Alderdice's clock, shoe last, and wooden nails

John Brookie and Agnes Alderdice
Anderson, my grandparents

Reverend Alderdice was a Scotch-Irishman who had emigrated from Ireland. After attending seminary, he was ordained as a Presbyterian minister. He traveled the circuit on horseback, ministering to towns too small to afford a full-time pastor. Ministers in those days had to be self-employed to be able to afford to preach. They sometimes received missionary boxes containing hand-me-down clothes. The faithful gave what they could afford. Most of the settlers were farmers, and if they didn't have money, they shared food. In his saddlebags, Grandpa carried equipment for making shoes, different sizes of shoe lasts, and tiny triangular wooden nails to fasten the soles to the shoe. I have one of the wooden shoe lasts and a bottle of the tiny nails from his saddlebags. I also have the mantle clock they had when they set up housekeeping.

John Brookie and Agnes had two children. The firstborn was Katie Bell, who died in June of 1885, at the age of 20 months, of black diphtheria. My father, John Hance Alderdice Anderson, was born on October 27, 1885, four months after the death of his sister. John Brookie passed away in 1889, leaving a widow and a small son to run the farm. Grandma did an amazing job.

When my father was young, there were still Indians that had chosen to stay in the area. Papa told us many stories about them and their way of life. He took us to areas where we could walk in the deeply worn toe paths the Indians had created by so many years of travel. We walked these paths down the hilly banks to the water of the Tippecanoe. When we prepared our fields for planting, we followed the plow and found arrowheads, stone axes, and other artifacts. This area had been the home of many generations of Native Americans.

The first five children in our family were raised much like our parents, as pioneer children. Everyone has their own memories; these are mine. I have written them as short stories, like windows looking back into my childhood.

# Acknowledgments

I wish to thank my cousin, Lt. Col. John M. Anderson, USAF Retired, author of "Scotch John Anderson." From his book I was able to gain information about our great-grandfathers.

Thanks to my dear daughter, Danna Gunther, for her many hours of editing. Now that the book is finished, she can go play with her grandson.

Special thanks to my grandson, Tim Gunther, for the hours he spent preparing the photos for "Papa Said." Tim is a professional artist who specializes in scientific illustration, graphic design, and fine art. Examples of his work can be seen at Gunthergraphics.biz.

Horse and buggy with Mamma and Papa on their wedding day

Mamma, Gladys Arrick Anderson

Papa, Dr. John Hance Alderdice Anderson

## Chapter 1

# Papa Said

It was a hot, humid August day. Our family had gathered in Indiana to attend the Anderson family reunion. I felt it was a good time to show my husband, two children, and six grandchildren where my family started.

We drove to the little town of Pittsburgh, Indiana, on the banks of the Wabash. The town is now gone. Of the old businesses, only "Sam's Fish House Restaurant" was left. A few of the old buildings still stood, but were either boarded up or used for different purposes. The old mill, the blacksmith shop, and the icehouse were gone.

Pittsburgh store with spring and horse tank in front

On the corner, where the old general store had stood, was a vacant lot. Next to the road, where there had been a spring-fed, wood-framed horse tank, there was now a round concrete watering tank fed by a pipe from the spring. Papa said he used to watch Indians ride their ponies here for water. People from all around bring jugs here to fill them with the sweet spring water. It is the best water in the area.

I was standing where I had stood with my father, and he with his father, watching my two children and their six children lean over to drink from the pure, clear spring water flowing from the pipe. I had a strong feeling of nostalgia.

Ruth with daughter and grandchildren
drinking from the spring


As I stood on the spot where the general store had been, my memory took me back in time and I began to tell my family the story of my childhood.

I remembered Papa bringing me here as a child. I could see the potbellied stove with it's chrome footrests on all sides. It was circled with old oak chairs where the old-timers sat exchanging stories and jokes. Well-used brass spittoons were strategically placed nearby. This was the gathering place for the farmers and old-timers in the area.

Papa was the only educated veterinarian for miles around. He knew, when he went into the store, he would be giving free medical advice to anyone who asked. He didn't mind until they tried to treat an animal themselves and waited until it was near death before calling him, expecting a miracle.

Bolts of fabric in calico, wool, linen, lace, and other materials, were laid out on one side of the store, along with needles, thread, yarn and almost any other thing needed by ladies in the community. On the opposite side of the store were shelves with canned goods, spices, and all kinds of staples. In front of the shelves stood two large glass cases filled with merchandise, including pocket watches, knives, guns and ammunition, and much more. I was more interested in the candy containers that adorned the top of the case. I knew the storeowner would treat me to whatever piece I chose.

At the back of the store were racks of garden tools, seeds, harnesses, and shelves filled with medicines for both man and animal.

About a block up the road stood the one-room schoolhouse where my brothers Raymond and Arthur, and sister Mabel had attended. Approximately a mile and a half further up the road was the old Anderson farm where my grandfather, father, my sisters Mabel and Esther, my brother Wayne and I, were born.

As I stood looking at the small two-story house sitting well back from the road, my head swam with memories of my childhood. This house, which had seemed huge to me as a child, was quite small. The country road was still gravel. The lane to the house was maybe 200 feet, not 400 feet, from the road.

We drove up the lane in two cars and parked. Not wanting to alarm the occupants, I went alone to the door. I explained why we had stopped, and the lady of the house was delighted to let us wander through and to hear my story about what the house was like before it had been remodeled.

There was no longer a springhouse off the kitchen, where we had kept the food refrigerated. In the springhouse there had been a large circular tub made of oak or hickory. Around the inside wall of the tub was a shelf approximately four inches below the water level. Crocks of butter, milk and cream along with meats and anything else that needed to be kept cold were covered with plates and set on this shelf in the water. Tall containers such as five-gallon cans of milk were set in the middle. The tub was filled with ice-cold spring water that had been piped into the house. Drains kept the water at the correct level.

When the weather was too muggy and hot in the summer, we used the wood-burning stove in the kitchen as little as possible, to avoid heating up the house. Instead, we used a 3-burner kerosene stove on an enclosed porch. Windows could be opened on all sides to let in any breath of air. Mamma would place a portable oven over two of the burners when she wanted to bake. We called this the summer kitchen.

As I stood in the main kitchen, I remembered it as it had been so many years ago. It was a large room that was kitchen, dining and living room. Centered on the west end of the room stood the wood-burning cook stove. To the left of the stove was a wood-box that had to be filled several times a day. The door to the mud room, back porch, and summer kitchen was to the right of the stove. Near the southwest corner of the kitchen was the door to our cellar. Our dining table with heavy oak bentwood chairs sat nearby. On the other end of the room, in the corner next to the parlor, stood a potbellied stove with a stovepipe that extended up through ceiling, one of the upstairs bedrooms, and out the roof. Whoever was lucky enough to be in that bedroom got some warmth from the pipe. That was the girls' room. The windows in this room looked out across the grassy area to the pasture, barn, and woods.

The kitchen was the only room in the house that was heated in winter. If we had company, more wood was put in the stove and the door was opened to the parlor. When spring brought warm weather, the heating stove was moved out and stored in a shed. The openings in the ceilings and upstairs floor were covered with decorative metal covers.

There were two rooms on the east end of the living area. One door led into a room that had been Grandma Anderson's library. When she had a stroke and could no longer climb stairs, this became her bedroom. After she passed away, it became my parents' bedroom.

The second door led into the parlor at the front of the house and opened onto the front porch. This was not a large room. On one side sat a horsehair sofa. In warm weather, I sometimes sat here with Papa and he would tell me stories. I loved his Indian stories. One particular story has stuck with me all my life. He told me about hungry Indians slipping into pastures, making a half-moon cut in the hind quarter of a cow, carving out a nice chunk of meat, and placing the hide back over the wound. Farmers might not notice this until it became infected and the cow died. Papa didn't blame the Indians. He felt sorry for them.

A painting used to hang on the wall to the left of the front door of the parlor. This painting fascinated me. It was a picture of an older lady working in the field, shocking wheat into sheaves. She was looking up at a tall man in a soldier's uniform, who was resting his rifle on the ground next to her. They looked so sad. I asked Papa about the picture.

He explained, "That picture is called, 'A Soldier's Farewell.' The soldier is going off to Europe to fight in the war. He has come home to say goodbye to his mother before he is shipped out."

"Did you fight in the war?" I asked.

"No, I had children, so they didn't call me," he explained. "I would have been in the next draft and would have gone in as a veterinarian in the cavalry, but the war ended before I had to go. My cousin George was in the Army, though, and he looked like that soldier."

"Do they let girls go into the Army?"

"No, Ruth, they only take men. They do allow women to go in as nurses." he answered.

Studying the picture I said, "When I grow up, if they have a war and they let women join, I will go."

Papa smiled at me and said, "I would hope you would, Purtsy. You are only five now. You may be lucky and there will not be another war. I hope there never is."

Two crank phones had hung on the wall of the kitchen, one for each of the two phone companies covering the area where my father's practice took him the most. We didn't have phone numbers. You called the Operator and asked to be connected to the party you wanted to reach. Each person had a specific ring. Our ring was two longs and a short. If you knew a person's ring, you would crank a full crank for a long and a half crank for a short. When the phone rang, it rang in everyone's home. You were supposed to listen for your ring and ignore the others. There were a lot of lonely housewives, so there were few secrets. You got to know everyone's ring.

Mamma could always find Papa if he was on a call. If the client had a phone, Mamma would call and ask if Dr. Anderson was there. If he had already left and the client didn't know where he was headed, someone on the line might speak up and say they had just seen him pass. Mamma would then know where to call to reach Papa. Sometimes, if no one spoke up, the Operator would volunteer that she had heard him promise to go to Mr. Cowger's farm. Everyone knew Papa and his car, one of the few in the area.

Looking out the back door of the kitchen, I could almost see my mother in a white dress that hung just below the tops of her high-button shoes, her raven-black hair pulled back in a bun, standing beside Papa's car with its polished brass kerosene lamps on either side of the windshield. She was a beautiful lady with deep brown eyes that seemed to light up when she smiled, and to turn black when she was angry. I could see Papa working his animals with his sheepdog, Shep. Papa was tall and slim, with hazel eyes and auburn hair, a strong, handsome man, devout in his faith, loved by everyone, and a strict father.

Our farm was known as a stud farm. Papa was known for his fine horses. He had the fastest horses in the area and would enter them in sulky races. When he was courting my mother, Papa would go early so he could drive slowly, giving them a chance to be alone together on their slow ride to church. Grandpa would wait until they had left. He and Grandma would follow in his buggy. He knew Papa's horse was trained to race and wouldn't let another horse pass him. This insured Grandpa that Mamma would get to church on time.

As we stepped out onto the little front porch, I remembered a time when I was three. Papa gathered all of us children together on the porch: Raymond age 8 1/2, Arthur 7, and Mabel 5. I was 3. In his most serious voice, Papa explained that one of our cows, White Legs, had just had a calf. Papa said, "White Legs is very protective of her baby and can be very dangerous. You are all to stay out of the pasture and away from that calf. Do you understand?"

Four voices answered in unison, "Yes, Papa."

When Papa was well out of earshot, Raymond began, "That sure is a pretty calf. I saw it. It sure is cute. You guys should see it. It's spotted black and white and it's lying just inside the pasture gate. Do you wanna see it?"

Remembering Papa's stern voice, I was the first to speak. "No, Papa said we shouldn't, because White Legs is mean."

"Aw, she's clear on the other side of the pasture. She probably can't even see that far. Besides, we could go in, pet the calf, and get out before she could get us."

"But Papa said," I persisted.

"Papa said, Papa said, is that all you know? You sissies can sit here, but I'm going to pet that calf!" With that, Raymond jumped off the porch and headed for the pasture. One by one, we followed.

Raymond was right. Just inside the gate was a little black and white calf. One by one, we climbed over the gate and gathered around to pet the beautiful animal. Suddenly I realized I was by myself. The others had left. Looking up, I saw an angry White Legs racing across the pasture toward me with her head down. To this day, I don't know how I got over that gate. I was running for the house as fast as my little legs would carry me. Looking back, I saw White Legs clear the gate, head down, and gaining on me.

Suddenly, out of nowhere, I saw Papa running toward me with a pitchfork in his hand, with Shep beside him. He dashed between me and the angry cow, ready to bring her down if necessary. Shep did her job, nipping at the cow's legs and barking. Papa didn't have to use the pitchfork.

I don't remember what Papa said to Raymond, but I am sure his actions spoke louder than words.

As we left the farm, I pointed out the field, which had been planted in corn, and told them the story that Mamma loved to tell about Raymond taking care of Mabel when she was 1 ½ years old.

## Chapter 2

# Stuck With Mabel

### 1919

It was a late-summer day in Indiana. A slight breeze was rustling the leaves of the huge sycamore tree in our front yard. The sun streaking through the trees made dancing shadow pictures on the lawn. The smell of fresh-baked bread wafted from the open windows of our farmhouse.

Five-year-old Raymond, with his bright red hair and freckled face, was chasing Arthur around and around the tree with a garter snake in his outstretched hand, laughing and shouting as they ran.

Arthur was the exact opposite of Raymond, a quiet sensitive child with thick black curly hair, a beautiful face, and a sweet, gentle disposition, always wanting to please. Raymond was constantly into trouble. Mamma said she thought he lay awake nights thinking of what mischief he could get into next. Hearing the commotion, Mamma stepped out onto the porch with Mabel in her arms. "Raymond, you stop teasing your brother this minute and put that snake out in the garden where it belongs! I don't want to have to tell Papa that you haven't been good boys while he was gone."

"Where is Papa?" Raymond asked as he made one last lunge at his brother with the snake before turning it loose in the garden.

"He has gone over to Aunt Mae's to help Floyd and George husk their corn. Next week the boys will come here to help Papa husk our corn.

"Raymond, Mabel just got up from her nap and I am busy baking bread. Will you please watch her? I need her out from under my feet for a while."

"All right, Mamma, but if she starts bawling, you get her back."

Mabel was 21 months old. As Mamma set her down, she happily accepted the hand her big brother offered. As she bounced down the steps, her beautiful red curls seemed to turn to gold in the sun.

Mamma returned to her bread making and the two brothers played with their little sister. It wasn't long, however, before Raymond became bored.

"Art," he said, "I'll tell you what. Let's get the wagon and take turns pulling each other. The one who rides has to hold Mabel. I ride first cause I'm the oldest, right?"

"Okay, Red, but you gotta promise you will pull me second. The last time we did this, you ran away and I didn't get a ride."

Raymond grinned. "Okay, I promise. You pull me over to the cornfield and I'll pull you back." Placing Mabel in the wagon, he climbed in behind her. Arthur picked up the handle and started off. It was a hard pull for a three-and-a-half-year-old, even though it was slightly downhill.

When they reached the cornfield, Arthur dropped the

handle and flopped down onto the cool grass, exhausted. Raymond dangled his legs over the side of the wagon, his mind going a mile a minute. "You know, if we cut through the cornfield, you could cool off in the creek. I'll give Mabel something to play with and she will be okay."

Reaching into the pocket of his bib overalls, he pulled out his slingshot and handed it to Mabel. Her blue eyes shone with delight as she smilingly accepted her brother's prize slingshot. "Now, you gotta promise me you won't get out of that wagon if I let you play with my slingshot. You promise?" Mabel's head bobbed up and down. Remembering a book about snakes his grandmother had in her library, he added, "Besides, there are spreading vipers in the creek. Do you know what a spreading viper is? It's a big snake that can spread out so big, it can swallow anybody." From the corner of his eye, he saw Arthur's hazel eyes open wide in alarm and smiled to himself. Mabel just smiled as she played with her new toy.

Raymond whispered, "Come on, Art, before she starts bawling." Off through the corn he ran, with Arthur following more slowly behind, having lost some of his enthusiasm.

Mabel grew tired of her toy and, realizing her brothers had left, she slid down from the wagon and headed into the cornfield.

When Raymond and Arthur returned to find an empty wagon, both boys were frightened. Arthur didn't hesitate. "I'm going to get Mamma ." Raymond was already racing back and forth through the corn when Arthur returned with Mamma, our hired girl Tracy, and John the hired man. Spreading out, they started searching through the

40-acre cornfield, calling to Mabel as they searched the rows.

Finally, after what must have seemed like a lifetime, John heard Mabel sobbing. Calling to the others, he followed the sound, picked her up, and carried her to her mother. Mabel's dirty face was streaked with tears as her arms reached for Mamma, who held her close and spoke softly as she tried to calm the frightened child.

When Mabel was calmed down, Mamma turned her attention to Raymond. "Young man, when your father comes home, he is going to hear about this! What if we hadn't found your little sister?"

"Aw, what's the big deal? I don't know why you were all so worried. They would have found her when they husked the corn."

# Chapter 3

# Our Hired Man

## Summer 1922

John Hankins was a hard-working, leather-skinned man in his late thirties. His tattered old hat with the earflaps tied across the top was dusty, dirty and sweat-stained. His big calloused hands showed the years of hard labor. He had just enough education to get by.

We all loved John, except Mamma, who didn't approve of some of his language and habits, such as chewing tobacco. "Such a filthy habit," she would say. He was careful not to take his Bull Durum tobacco pouch out of his jacket pocket in front of Mamma or to chew in the house. He sure was a crack shot when he was outside, though. I think he could hit a bug on the move five feet away. That was something to see. He watched his cursing around Mamma and the girls, but Raymond learned a few choice words, which he only used when Mamma and Papa were out of earshot.

John was like part of our family. He had worked for Papa and Grandma for years. He loved and admired Papa and respected Mamma. Papa would remind Mamma that

John was a hard worker and devoted to all of us. "Good hired men are hard to find," he would remind her. "If they are worth their salt, they usually get a place of their own." She knew he was right.

Not only did John do regular daily chores, such as milking, slopping the hogs, feeding the animals, cleaning the barn and chicken house, and chopping wood, but there was plowing, planting, fertilizing, cultivating, harvesting, shelling corn, and storing the harvest.

Papa worked right alongside John when he was home. They were up before dawn to do the milking, feed the animals, and put them out in the pasture before coming in to breakfast. After breakfast, Papa would leave to make his calls while John carried on with the farm work. Papa's veterinary practice was growing, taking him away from the farm more and more, leaving John with more responsibility. As soon as Papa returned, he would check his animals and continue working until dark.

When John finished his work, he would wash up outside, weather permitting. We kept a basin on a stand by the pump. On the framework of this stand was hook for a towel and another hook for a chipped enamel cup that everyone used. John would rinse out the cup, fill it with water from the pump, rinse out his mouth, spit it out, and take a big long drink of the cold spring water. He was careful to stamp the dirt and manure from his boots before stepping onto the back porch and into the mudroom where he removed them on the paper provided. Taking off his coat and hat, he hung them on the coat rack next to the kitchen door, and joined the family for supper.

When supper was over, John would often play checkers

with Raymond and Arthur, or just entertain us with his tall tales, jokes and funny songs or poems.

One evening, after supper, Raymond motioned for me to follow him into the parlor. Loving the attention and secrecy, I followed. Looking toward the door to be sure no one had followed, Raymond whispered. "I'll give you something really good if you will do something for me."

"What do I have to do?" I asked. "Will I get in trouble?"

"Nah, I just want to kinda play a trick on John and I want you to help. I'll keep John busy playing checkers while you go out in the mudroom and get the chewing tobacco out of his jacket pocket. Bring it right back here and put it under the sofa, right here." he said, showing me where to put it. "Wait until Mamma puts Esther to bed, cause if she sees you it will spoil the trick. If you don't let anyone see, I'll give you some tobacco. It's good stuff."

I was excited about being a partner with my big brother. When Mamma picked up Esther and headed for the bedroom, Raymond asked John to play him a game of checkers. As they sat down at the table, Raymond nodded to me and I slipped out the door to the mudroom. I had to stand on tiptoes to reach the jacket pocket, but I got the tobacco, hid it in my full skirt, slipped back to the parlor, and placed it where I had been told. At the age of three, I had committed my first and only crime.

When Raymond saw me come in, he said, "Art, you can play the first game and I will play the next." The checkers had been set up and Arthur was surprised and happy that he got to go first. Raymond followed me into the parlor, took the pouch, and, opening it, he gave me a leaf of tobacco. Shoving the tobacco in his pocket he returned to the table.

I put the leaf he had given me in my mouth. It tasted sort of sweet with a bite. I don't remember if I swallowed it, but I probably did, having had no previous experience or instructions.

I went to the table to watch the checker game.

Standing at John's elbow, my head was just above the edge as I watched. Three-year-olds get lots of attention without trying. Mabel was feeling very left out. She was a tall, skinny, five-year-old with a cameo-like face, sprinkled with freckles and framed by beautiful red curls. She kept pestering John to get his attention, and he would tease her back.

Finally the game was finished and John turned his attention to Mabel. "Do you want to hear a poem about Mabel?" he asked. With John, an answer wasn't necessary.

> I once knew a girl named Mabel.
> She got up to dance on the dining room table.
> She blushed very red when the gentlemen said
> Look at the legs on the table.

Everyone laughed except Mabel and Mamma, who had just come into the room. Mamma could say as much with a look as with words. Her dark brown eyes snapping, she said, "I don't think much of your poetry, John."

John decided it was time to check on the stock. That was the last of John's poetry, at least around us girls, but Raymond was a fast learner with a good memory, and the poem followed Mabel throughout her childhood.

## Chapter 4

# Dry Grass

## August 1922

"**M**abel, why must you and your sister always fight with each other?" Mamma scolded. "Why don't the two of you go outside and play? Your little sister is sick and I am tired of having to leave her to break up fights between you two."

"It's too hot outside," Mabel complained. "I want to play with my doll."

"Can I go out and play with the lamb?" I asked.

"Yes, if you stay in the shade near the house," Mamma answered. "Be sure to close the screen as you go out, or we will be eaten up by mosquitoes."

The minute I stepped out the door, I heard the bleat of my lamb, Fluff, as she came running to me with Shep following close behind. Fluff didn't need to be penned up during the day; Shep would not let anything happen to her. Normally, we were not allowed to make pets of the animals because Papa didn't want us to become attached to an animal that might someday be served on our table. Fluff was an exception however. She had been orphaned and I got to feed her from a bottle. Papa said someday she would have babies of her own.

When I stepped off the porch and my bare feet hit the dry grass, I stepped quickly as if moving fast would stop the burning heat in the ground. Where there was no grass, the bare ground was cracked like broken glass, from lack of rain.

I ran as fast as I could, Shep and Fluff following close behind, to the shade of the sycamore tree in our front yard. There was very little breeze blowing, but what there was could be felt in the shade of that giant tree. I sat with my two best friends, my back against the tree, looking up through the leaves at a robin's nest. A red squirrel scolded as he jumped from branch to branch. In the distance, I could hear the call of the whippoorwill followed by an answering call in the distance.

I didn't hear Papa's car as he drove up the lane. "Purtsy, what are you doing sleeping out here? You are going to be eaten up by mosquitoes," Papa said as he picked me up and carried me to the porch.

"Mamma said I could play out here cause Mabel don't like me and Esther is sick." I explained.

"Mamma didn't say Mabel doesn't like you, now, did she?"

"No, but she don't like me. She hits me when Mamma isn't there." I answered.

Setting me down on the porch, he removed his dirty boots and stopped to wash up at the washstand on the porch before going into the house. I stood watching him scrub his hands and arms, toss the water into the yard, dip clean water into the basin, and wash his face. Taking the towel from the hook on the wall behind the washstand, he dried himself and went into the house with me close behind. Mamma was there with a smile and a kiss to greet him.

"Mother, you look tired," he said as he held her close. "How is Esther?"

"I think she is better. She is sleeping now. Dr. Crampton was here. He gave me some new medicine and said he believes she has colitis. I have been giving her tea and he said to boil her water."

"Why don't you get some rest, Gladys, while the boys are still at school? I'll take the girls with me. I want to check the north pasture and the crops. Come along, Mabel. You and Ruth can help me while your mother rests."

I was always eager to go with Papa. Mabel stepped off the porch and I jumped off behind her. Papa took our hands as we took off past the garden where Tracy was picking beans for supper.

"Hi, Tracy, you better not stay out in this heat too long. I don't want you having a heat stroke. You could fry eggs on a rock, it's so hot. I told Gladys to rest. When the boys get home, will you try to keep them quiet and see that they get their chores done?"

"I certainly will, Dr. Anderson. I am almost finished picking the beans."

We passed between the barn and the woods, walking toward the pasture. Trying to keep up with Papa's long stride was difficult. I half ran and half walked. Papa looked down at me and asked, "Are you tired, Purtsy? Here, I'll carry you for awhile." Reaching down, he lifted me into his strong arms. "How are you doing, Mabel? Am I going too fast?"

"No, Ruth is just a sissy. She just likes to be carried."

21

"Remember, Ruth is only three; you are five and your legs are longer." We had passed the woods and were walking through the north pasture. The grass was burned brown from the hot sun and no rain. I could hear the dry brittle grass crunching under Papa's feet. Circling the woods, we returned through the corn field. Papa pulled off an ear of corn and pulled down the husks: Our corn crop was gone. We continued on past the soybean field. Papa pulled a few bean pods: they weren't filled out. We headed back to the house.

We entered the house quietly, but Mamma was up, busily helping Tracy with supper. "How did the pasture look?" she asked as she removed two apple pies from the oven. "Was there any grass left? It's been so long since we had any rain. If we hadn't carried water to the garden, it would have burned up."

"The pasture is dried up. If we don't get rain soon, we will have to sell most of the cattle and sheep. I don't know who would buy them, though; everyone is in the same boat. Feed is so high. I will probably have to ship them to Chicago to the Stockyards. With the price of beef so low now, it will hardly pay to ship them. I hate to think of those good milk cows being butchered. We must continue to pray for rain. We are fortunate that we have a good well. Several of my clients' wells are drying up. As hot and humid as it is, there must be rain somewhere."

"Well, Hance, you could butcher one of the steers, and Tracy and I will can the meat. At least we will have enough to eat. We have a good garden. Tracy and I can put up enough vegetables and fruit to last a year, if need be. Many people are less fortunate."

When Papa said grace before supper, and again at evening

prayer after Bible reading that night, he asked God to send the much needed rain. He never forgot to thank God for our many blessings and to pray for those who had less than us. Papa always ended his prayers with, "Thy will be done. In Jesus name we pray, Amen."

That night I was awakened by loud claps of thunder followed by rain on our shingled roof. God had answered Papa's prayer. I was impressed. I figured Papa had a direct line to God. It was too little, too late, to save our corn and beans, but the pasture came back to life.

## Chapter 5

# Over The River To Grandpa's

## Late summer 1922

Papa had washed and polished his automobile ready for our trip to Grandpa's. The polished brass kerosene lamps on either side of the windshield were reflected on the shiny jet-black finish of the car. Papa only polished the car when we were going to church or to Grandpa's. It didn't make any difference anyway. The minute he got onto the gravel roads, the car was dirty again.

Papa had carried two baskets of food Mamma had prepared, and stored them in the boot of the car. Mabel and I had our Sunday dresses on. Mamma had curled Mabel's hair. It hung in golden red curls down to her shoulders. Raymond and Arthur were dressed in their knee breeches, ready to go. As they stepped out the door, Mamma called after them. "Now you boys be good. Don't get dirty."

"Ruth, you are next. Let's get your hair curled." Mabel was lucky. Her hair was not thick like mine. I squirmed and complained all the time Mamma brushed, combed, and curled it around her finger. "Now you and Mabel sit here until I get Esther dressed. I don't want you to get dirty before we leave."

"Cut it out Red!" Mamma stepped to the door to see why Arthur was upset with his brother. Raymond was throwing clods of dirt at Arthur who had, so far, been able to dodge them. Losing patience, he decided to retaliate by catching them and throwing them back.

"Raymond, stop tormenting your brother. If you boys get dirty before we even get started, you are going to get a spanking. Hance, I am sending the boys out to the car. Please keep an eye on them or I never will get ready to go."

Papa in his stern voice said, "You boys get in the car while I help your mother. I don't want to hear one thing out of either of you. Do you understand?"

"Yes" they answered in unison.

Papa stepped up on the porch. "Mother, it is clouding up. We may run into rain. Can I do anything to help you? We should be on our way. I will get the girls in the car and start it. I see you are almost finished with Esther."

"Good. Thank you, dear. I will be right out," she answered with a deep sigh. Getting five children ages one to nine ready to go anyplace was quite a task.

Papa lifted me into the car next to Arthur. Taking Mabel's hand, he helped her in beside me. "Now you boys stay on your side of the seat," Papa ordered. "Raymond, there will be no teasing or tormenting of your brother and sisters. Do you understand me? I have to keep my mind on driving and I would hate to have to stop to take care of you."

"I'm coming, Hance," Mamma called as she stepped out the door with Esther in her arms. Papa reached up and took

Esther as Mamma stepped off the porch. Taking Mamma's arm, he assisted her up into the seat of the car and handed her the baby. "You do have the food baskets stored away, don't you?" she asked.

"Everything is taken care of," he said as he stepped to the front of the car. Leaning over, he cranked the engine until it started, removed the crank, stored it under the seat, and climbed in. He adjusted two silver bars that stuck out from the steering shaft, and we were on our way.

I loved going to Grandpa Arrick's, but I hated the long drive. I always got carsick. It was a good twenty miles to Grandpa's over narrow, bumpy, country roads used mostly by horse-drawn buggies, wagons, and farm equipment. Its graveled surface was rough and rutted. Papa's car left a rolling cloud of dust behind us.

Everyone we passed knew our car and would wave or shout a greeting. Frequently a farmer would flag us down and ask Papa to take a look at one of their animals. This day was no exception.

A magnificent pair of workhorses approached us, pulling a loaded wagon. Papa steered to the side of the road to allow them to pass. As they came alongside, the farmer driving the team drew back on the reins and stepped down. He was a huge man, covered with dust and perspiration. His disarming smile wrinkled the leathery skin of his face. His bib overalls were faded and stained. He wore an old brimmed hat with a dark greasy-looking stain spreading out from the band around the crown, making the band look much wider than it really was.

Removing his hat, he greeted Mamma and then said, "Dr. Anderson, I have been meaning to call you, but just don't seem to get around to it. I have some young heifers that need dehorning. While you are at it, I guess I should have you vaccinate my hogs too. Do you think you could do it Sunday? I won't be in the field that day."

"No, Frank, I don't work on Sunday except for emergencies. If you will have them penned up, I think I can take care of them early Monday morning, unless there is some emergency. In that case, I will call you."

"That will be fine, Doc. I'll have them ready and one of the boys will be there to help. It's nice seeing you again, Mrs. Anderson. Maybe Doc will bring you along and you can visit with my wife. She gets pretty lonesome out here. I'm sure you know how that is."

Mamma smiled as she answered. "I would like that, Frank. Tell Martha I will be there unless one of the children is sick."

Frank replaced his hat, climbed back up on the wagon, and with a smile and a wave he snapped the reins and drove on.

Papa pulled back on the road. By this time, we were all getting restless. With the four of us wedged into the back seat on a hot day, I became more and more uncomfortable. The rain, of which Papa had spoken, became more threatening.

Papa said, "I think we had better stop and put on the rain curtains, don't you, Gladys?"

"I don't know dear. You know how driving affects Ruth. I am afraid being closed in, in this heat and humidity, it might be worse. Let's wait until the rain starts."

It wasn't long before huge drops of rain were hitting the windshield. Papa pulled over and he and Mamma put up curtains in the front seat while we put them up in the back. There were brass grommets on all sides of the curtains. These were fit over two-piece brass latches on all sides of the windows. The grommets were hooked over these and by turning the end of the latch, the curtains were held tightly in place. They kept the rain out, but also the breeze.

Knowing how riding affected me, my parents tried to keep me interested in other things. Mamma would point out where Papa had delivered a calf. She would say, "If you watch, maybe you will see it in the pasture with its mother," or she would point out where some first cousin, once removed, lived. It didn't help. In fact, watching the scenery go by made it worse. Lightening cut across the sky, followed by rolling thunder. The patter of the rain on the roof had a soothing affect, but I was getting sicker by the minute. The ruts in the road had filled with water, splashing as we drove.

"When will we get there, Papa? I don't feel very good. My stomach feels funny."

"It won't be long, Ruth. Watch for the big bridge over the river. When you see that, you will know we are halfway there."

"It better be soon before Ruth pukes all over everybody," Raymond interjected. "She is turning green."

We had reached the bridge. The rain had stopped and the sun was trying to break through the clouds. Papa stopped beside the road, removed his window curtains, shook the rain from them, and stored them in the door pockets. Opening my door, he lifted me out and carried me to the bridge. The rain had cooled the air. My stomach was rolling. Papa set me on my feet. Holding onto my hand, he walked with me on the bridge.

"This is the Tippecanoe River, Ruth. When the Indians

lived here, they would put their birch wood canoes into the water and they could go all the way to the ocean from here. This river meets the Wabash River down near Lafayette, and from there it flows into the Ohio River, down to the Mississippi River. The Mississippi flows into the ocean."

"There is a funny story about where the river got its name. The way I heard it, this big Indian chief took his little son out in the canoe. The boy stood up and his father said, "Sit down son, you tippy canoe." I loved Papa's stories, but right at that time I chose to get rid of my breakfast. Papa wiped my face with his handkerchief and we walked back toward the car. When we reached the end of the planks, Papa picked me up so I wouldn't get my Sunday shoes dirty.

I was feeling a little better when we got back to the car. As we drove across the bridge, our wheels on the wooden planks sounded a clump, clump, clump that echoed across the river.

We finally pulled into Grandpa's yard. Grandpa wore an old tattered straw hat which covered his curly red hair. I was the first out of the car and running to him for the big hug I knew I would get. Grandpa was carrying a bucket, which he placed on the ground as he leaned over to catch me. Grandpa's face lit up and his blue eyes sparkled as he lifted me into his arms. Over his shoulder, I saw Winona, Mamma's thirteen-year-old sister, rushing out to greet us. Since Grandma's death two years earlier, Winona and Grandpa's half-sister, Aunt Sadie, had kept house for Grandpa.

Grandpa Carmi Arrick

Papa greeted his father-in-law and said, "Gladys tells me you need help milling some lumber."

"That's right, Hance. One of the neighbors ask me to build a chest of drawers for his wife for Christmas. With the way crops have been, I was glad for the work. I had cut down a cherry tree, but hadn't had anyone to help mill it." Grandpa was a fine finish-carpenter. He could build anything.

Mamma and Winona, followed by Mabel, carried the food baskets into the house. The boys took off in a run for fear I would want to go with them or Papa would ask them to look after me.

I followed Papa and Grandpa out to the edge of the woods. Behind a split-rail fence stood a huge circular saw which was housed in a shed-type building with three sides. Grandpa had cut down a large wild cherry tree and had removed the branches. He had attached logging chains to the tree, hooked it up to a team of draft horses, and pulled it from the woods to the mill. It had been lifted up onto logs to dry, ready to be cut into manageable lengths.

Papa stood me on a stump behind the split-rail fence and ordered me to stay there if I wanted to watch. "Sawing wood can be very dangerous, even for grownups," he said.

Grandpa lifted a long, two-man saw from a beam where it hung, stepped over the tree, and set the saw across it at the spot where he wanted to cut. He gripped the wooden handle on his end of the saw. Papa, on the other side of the tree, grasped the other handle. They began to saw. Back and forth, back and forth, they pushed and pulled as the saw made its own rhythmic music. Sawdust was piling up under the tree.

When the tree had been cut into manageable lengths, Grandpa hung his saw back on the wooden pegs in the beam. Papa placed heavy ropes around the first log and attached the hook of a block and tackle that hung from the beam above. Papa pulled the rope through grooved wheels of the pulley, lifting the great log off the ground. Grandpa guided the log onto the belt that fed the saw. The ropes and tackle were removed.

Grandpa started the gasoline-powered saw. The loud chug, chug of the motor drowned the voices of the working men. Grandpa fed the log to the blade. The great blade sang as it sliced through the log, throwing sawdust as it cut. Papa, at the other end, lifted the boards off as they were cut, and stacked them out of the way. The blade was stopped, the log returned, repositioned, and the process repeated until the entire log was cut into planks. Those planks were stacked and would be sorted and cut to desired sizes later.

The air hung heavy with humidity. The sun beating down on the tin roof of the mill made working difficult. Both men frequently reached for the crockery jug of water.

By the time the third log had been cut up, both men were dripping wet with perspiration. They had removed their hats and were wiping their faces with handkerchiefs when the sound of the dinner bell rang out across the yard. Grandpa shut off the engine and we hurried into the house. I had to run to keep up.

When we reached the house, Grandpa and Papa cleaned up at the pump. I rushed in to see what we were having for dinner. The table had been set. A huge platter of fried chicken sat at one end with a large dish of mashed potatoes and a boat of gravy. At the other end was a dish of green beans from our garden, homemade bread Mamma had brought, and a glass pitcher of fresh lemonade with thin slices of lemon floating in it. On the sideboard sat two fresh apple pies Mamma had made this morning, before we got up.

When everyone was seated, heads bowed and hands folded, Grandpa asked the blessing. The food was passed and everyone was eating when Grandpa turned to Mamma, smiled and said, "Dot, you cook like your mother." I was too young to understand why his voice broke and he was wiping away tears from his eyes.

Chapter 6

# The Huckster Man

## Spring 1923

It was a beautiful spring morning. The birds were returning from their winter homes in the south. I could hear the cooing of the mourning dove, calling from the woods. The whippoorwill sang, "Whip-poor-will," out across the pasture. A cardinal, in it's brilliant red plumage, perched on a branch of the maple tree and sang, "Peter! Peter! "

The grass was still wet with dew as I stepped off the porch following Mamma. As I looked toward the woods, it was like looking at a beautiful painting. The snow-white flowers of the dogwood trees, interspersed with the red purple of the redbud, stood against the many shades of green in the woods. There were a variety of trees, including tulip, beech, hickory, black walnut, red and white oak, and maple, which were beginning to leaf out.

I loved spring. Everything was new and clean. Every place you looked was beauty. Wildflowers were popping up everywhere. After being inside most of the time during the long winter, I felt like a bird released from a cage.

I ran to catch up with Mamma. She walked past the newly plowed and disked garden area, next to which was a split-rail enclosure. This was the birthing pen for a huge black-and-white sow. Mamma had made several trips to check on her already this morning.

"Is the pig sick?" I asked.

"No, she is going to have babies and some pigs aren't good mothers. I have to watch her to be sure she doesn't kill them. She killed her babies the last time. If she kills her pigs this time, we will have to butcher her."

"Ruth, do you want to help me plant the garden? Mama asked. You are almost four, now. I think you are big enough to learn to plant beans and peas, don't you? I can work in the garden and watch the sow at the same time. Run get your sunbonnet."

"I want to watch for the Huckster Man."

"You will hear his bell when he gets here. Mabel and Esther are playing in the house. You can't stay in there; you know how you and Mabel fuss. If you stay here with me, I won't have to run in there to break up a fight. This is a good time to get some work done while Wayne is napping. Run along now and don't slam the door or you will wake the baby."

Farm families always went to town on Saturday night. Stores stayed open until 10 or 11. It was a time to stock up for the week ahead, but just as important, it was our social life. Mamma and Papa knew everyone. Mamma caught up on all the births, deaths, operations, weddings and scandals. Ladies exchanged recipes and home remedies. Papa would walk into a store and farmers would gather around him, laughing as they exchanged stories and jokes. He loved a good story. This was also a good chance for the farmers to get free medical advice.

During the week, we depended on the Huckster for anything Mamma had run out of or had forgotten at the store. The huckster came once a week and carried lace, needles, buttons, elastic, thread, and vegetable seeds, as well as staples such as canned goods, peanut butter, flour, sugar, salt and most anything a housewife would need. Mamma didn't buy her spices from the Huckster; she waited for the Raleigh man. Mamma said Raleigh spices were the best. Unlike the Huckster, the Raleigh man came once a month, but when he came, kids came running at the sound of his bell. He knew each of us by name and we would each be given a whole stick of Juicy Fruit gum by the smiling man.

By the time I returned with my sunbonnet, Mamma had started to plow long straight furrows in the soft black soil with her two-handled garden plow. Setting the plow aside, she pulled the bonnet on over my curls, tying it under my chin. " Now you keep this on. That sun is hot and your skin will burn," she said. The bonnet cupped out over my round freckled face and the back draped down over my neck.

Picking up her hand plow, Mamma resumed her plowing. I walked in the row behind her as the furrow opened up. The soil in the furrow was cool on my bare feet. I watched for arrowheads as Mamma turned the soil. A red-breasted robin snatched up an earthworm that had been uncovered and was trying to dig back into the ground.

"Now Ruth, you can plant the beans. See the little spot on the top of the bean? That is the eye of the bean, where the new bean will sprout and come up through the ground. You must place the bean with the eye so it will come up straight. See how I do it?" she said as she placed one bean after another in the row. "See how far apart I have set them? Now, you try it."

I squatted down beside the row, carefully placing the beans just as Mamma had done. "That's very good, Ruth. You finish the beans while I make the mounds for the melons and cucumbers. When you finish, I will show you how to plant the peas. While you plant the peas, I will cover the beans."

Mamma picked up her hoe and started mounding soil up to form a round hill. She tapped the top of the hill gently with the flat side of the hoe, moved on about four feet and repeated the process until she had a row of mounds. Reaching into her apron pocket, she brought out packets of seeds. Choosing the melon she wanted to plant first, she placed the other packets back in her pocket.

I had finished the beans and went over to watch Mamma plant the melons.

"See, I put six seeds in each hill. Can you guess why?" she asked as she placed them in a circle and dusted a light covering of soil over them.

"No," I said, shaking my head.

"Well, we know the birds will get some of them, so we share. We hope they won't get them all."

I heard the sound of a car coming up our drive, with its bell ringing loudly until it came to a stop near the edge of the garden. "It's the Huckster Man," I shouted, as I ran to see what he had. Maybe Mamma would buy a stick of candy for me. Mamma leaned her hoe against the fence as she followed me.

"Ruth, you run get my pocketbook so I can pay for the things I need," Mamma said as she greeted the Huckster Man.

"Good Morning, Mrs. Anderson. What can I get for you today?"

"Well, I would like to see what you have in flower seeds," she said.

Mamma was looking through the packets of seeds when I returned with her pocketbook. She chose several packets. Then, pulling a slip of paper from her apron pocket, she started looking through his supplies and picking out what she needed.

Suddenly the peaceful quiet of our yard was broken by the shrill squeal of a little pig. Mamma dropped everything and ran toward the pigpen. The Huckster man ran after her, shouting, "Mrs. Anderson, don't go in that pen! That sow might attack you!"

All I could hear was the cry of the dying pig. Lifting her long skirts, Mamma jumped the rail fence, grabbing the hoe as she went. With the hoe, she drove the sow into an adjoining enclosure and closed the gate. She then retrieved the remaining pigs.

I think the Huckster Man was more shaken than Mamma. She paid him, gathered up her purchases, and thanked him for his concern. "Here, Ruth, you take these things into the house while I go out to the shed and get a basket for the little pigs. You can help take care of them. They will have to be fed often, just like babies, until they are big enough to eat on their own." Secretly, I was glad the sow didn't want her pigs. I loved taking care of baby animals.

I was so proud of Mamma, the minute Papa got home

I rushed to greet him and was talking so fast, Papa said, "Slow down, Purtsy. I can't understand a word you are saying."

I took a deep breath and said, "You should have seen Mamma! She wasn't scared of that old sow! She jumped over that fence and she whacked that old sow with her hoe and she chased it away from the babies. She was so brave, she wasn't scared a bit, but the Huckster Man was!"

Papa looked at Mamma. "Gladys, is that true? Did you do such a foolish thing? If that sow had turned on you, she could have killed you. No pigs are worth your taking such a chance." Papa sounded cross, but I was still proud of Mamma.

Mamma smiled her disarming smile as she stood on tiptoes to give him a kiss. "I am still cross with you," he said as he gathered her into his arms and returned the kiss. "Don't ever do anything like that again."

"Don't I get credit for saving the pigs?" she teased. Papa shook his head and smiled. He couldn't stay cross with Mamma.

———————— ✑ ————————

## Chapter 7

# Our Fire Extinguisher

It was a hot, muggy day. Early in the morning, Mamma had drawn all the shades in the house to keep the hot sun out. She prepared breakfast on the kerosene stove in the summer kitchen. After breakfast, she heated a dishpan of water on one burner of the kerosene stove and a teakettle on the other burner for scalding the clean dishes. An empty dishpan sat on a counter to the left of the stove. After the dishes were washed, they would be stacked in the empty pan and rinsed with the hot water from the teakettle.

"Mabel," Mamma called, "bring the comb and I will curl your hair while the water heats. By the time I have finished curling your hair, the dishwater will be warm and you can wash the dishes for me while I comb Ruth's hair." Mabel came running, comb in hand. She hadn't yet discovered that washing dishes was work.

When Mamma finished combing Mabel's hair, she got up and moved a stool over in front of the stove, checked the water temperature, and put a cake of lye soap and a dish cloth in the dishpan. Mabel climbed up on the stool, rubbed soap into the cloth, and proceeded to wash the dishes and set them in the pan.

Mamma sat down to comb my hair and the phone rang. By the time she got back, the teakettle was singing. Mamma rinsed the first batch of dishes and set them out to drain on a towel while she went to the pump to refill the kettle. Before she got to the pump, the phone rang again. She set the kettle down and hurried to answer it.

I had been standing, holding the celluloid comb. I was bored. I climbed up on the stool beside Mabel. Looking down into the open burner, I was fascinated by the bright leaping flames. I decided to see what would happen if I held my comb over them. The instant the heat hit the celluloid comb, it burst into flame in my hand. Screaming, I let it drop into the burner, and flames shot almost to the ceiling.

Mabel dumped her dishwater into the burner, putting out the flame before Mamma reached the kitchen in response to my shrieks. My sister was a hero.

The stove and kitchen were a mess, but Mamma was so glad no one was hurt, she didn't seem to mind. Mamma told everyone who came to the house how I had tried to burn the house down and Mabel had saved it and maybe our lives. Mabel got a lot of well-deserved praise. For a six-year-old she had shown unusually quick thinking.

This had not been a good day for me, and when I saw Dr. Crampton driving up the lane, I knew it wasn't going to improve.

Papa said there was whooping cough going around and the doctor thought we children should be vaccinated. Dr. Crampton was not the most gentle of doctors. He laid me across his knees, and without explanation or warning, thrust a needle into my back. I jumped, breaking the needle, angering Dr. Crampton. He had to pull it out, get a new needle and give me another shot. I have a feeling that needle had been used too many times and needed replacing, anyway.

Dr. Crampton was quite a character. I heard Papa telling about him sitting in his upstairs office with his friend, the poet, James Whitcomb Riley. When they got together, they liked to have a few drinks. One day, after a few too many, they decided to see who could spit tobacco juice most accurately. Opening the window over the sidewalk, they took aim at chosen passersby. I never heard who won.

## Chapter 8

# Visual Education

## Summer 1923

"Hey, Art, ya wanna play marbles?" Raymond called to his brother as Arthur headed for the kitchen with an armful of wood.

Mamma said for me to tell you to help fill the wood-box, Red. When we finish, I will play you."

Raymond jumped up and ran to the woodpile, filled his arms with the newly split wood, and followed Arthur into the kitchen.

As the boys came out the door onto the back porch, letting the screen slam behind them, Raymond whispered to his brother. "I'll make you a deal. You are really good at marbles, better than me. Let's play for keeps."

Arthur knew his brother well. He knew if he were so much better than Raymond, his marble bag wouldn't be only half the size of Raymond's. "You know, Papa said no more playing Keepers. You got in trouble for playing that at school when Mabel found out and tattled. That is gambling and we aren't supposed to gamble. I think it says so in the Bible."

"Oh, it does not! You just say that because you are afraid I might win one of your precious marbles. That's okay. If you are so scared, maybe you should go play dolls with the girls." Raymond watched Arthur out of the corner of his eye to make sure his comment had it's desired effect.

"I'm not afraid to play you. I'll play, but I won't use my red agate. I know that's why you want to play for keeps."

"Okay, you don't have to play the red agate." Raymond knew just how far to push Art. If he wanted to play, he had to compromise.

Raymond led the way to the front of the house, out of sight of the clothesline. They chose a bare dusty spot on the side of the drive. The big maple tree beside the drive provided shade from the hot summer sun. Raymond picked up a dead stick from under the tree and drew a circle in the dirt. They each placed marbles in the circle. Mabel was sitting on the porch, playing with her doll. I started to follow my brothers when I heard Mamma calling. "Ruth, come into the house. I want you to play with Esther while I bring in the clothes from the line."

Esther was almost two. We sat on the floor and I helped her stack blocks. As we stacked them, I would show her the picture of animals on the side of the blocks and got her to tell me what each animal said.

Mamma returned from the line with her arms full of fresh-smelling clothes. She smiled as she walked through the kitchen to the bedroom and dropped them on the bed and began to fold them. The bedroom was on the front of the house. The open windows looked out across the front lawn to the road beyond and allowed any breeze blowing to pass through the house.

"John Raymond," I heard her call from the open window, "You come in here this minute!"

Raymond appeared at the kitchen door, stomped the dust from his shoes and entered, being careful not to let the screen door slam behind him. This was unusual for Raymond when he hadn't been reminded.

"What did you do?" I whispered.

"Shut up," he snarled as he shoved past me into the bedroom. Mamma was waiting, looking very cross. When Mamma was cross, her big brown eyes seemed almost black. She closed the door behind him and I knew I wasn't going to hear what was said.

After some time, the door opened and Raymond stepped out with his lips pressed tightly together and a scowl on his face. Mamma was close behind. Stomping across the room to the stove, Raymond picked up the shovel from the ash bucket and went out, slamming the screen door behind him this time. "You clean that shovel before you bring it back in, young man," Mamma called after him.

"Where's Raymond going?" I asked.

"Never you mind. He has a job to take care of," Mamma answered as she returned to the bedroom. I knew better than to pursue the subject.

Not satisfied with the answer, however, I ran to the window to see what a job was. Looking out across the front porch, I saw Raymond head for the big maple tree. He leaned over, scooped something up off the lawn, and headed for the outhouse.

You learn something every day. I don't know how old I was before I learned that there were other uses for the word "job."

*Chapter 9*

# The Old Windmill

## Spring 1924

Home on the farm, with windmill

The rhythmic patter of a March rain beat down on the roof and splashed against our kitchen windows. A fire blazed in the kitchen stove, and the fragrance of freshly baked bread permeated the air. Kerosene lamps in wall sconces lit the room in a warm, soft glow.

Papa, sitting at his roll top desk, was logging in the calls he had made today. Laying his book aside, he stood up and crossed the room. "Gladys, I am going out to check the stock before this storm gets any worse." Following him to the door, I watched him put on his slicker and cap. I stood in the door of the mudroom as he slipped into his rubber knee-high boots.

Patting me on the head, Papa said, "You go back in, Ruth, and close the door. You are letting the cold air in. I'll be back soon." I closed the door and heard the outside door slam. I rushed to the window and watched the shadowy figure of my father sloshing through the muddy yard. His path was lighted by the kerosene lantern he carried.

Suddenly, the storm intensified. The rain came down in sheets. The wind, which had been blowing lightly, became a whirling, threatening monster, tearing at our little frame house. Lightning seemed to split the sky open, followed by loud claps of thunder. I was glad Papa was home. I was never afraid when he was there. I watched from the window, hoping to see Papa coming back. The flashing lightening lit up the whole yard and barn.

It's a good thing you boys filled the wood-box before it started raining. It wouldn't be any fun doing it now." Mamma said.

"It wasn't any fun after school, either," Raymond whispered to Arthur.

"What did you say Raymond?" Mamma asked.

Raymond kicked his brother under the table and answered sweetly. "I said no, it wouldn't be any fun."

"Ruth, get away from that window," Mamma ordered. "You could be struck by lightening!" Reluctantly I obeyed and waited at the door for Papa. Everyone was gathered in the big kitchen. Raymond and Arthur were playing checkers at the kitchen table. Mabel was playing with Esther on the floor by the old potbellied stove. Mamma was feeding her bread starter.

"Are we having pancakes for breakfast?" I asked.

"Maybe, if you are a good girl."

I knew this meant yes.

Hearing the outside door slam, I rushed to open the kitchen door. Papa was removing his muddy boots on paper beside the door, and hanging his dripping coat and hat on pegs above them. He hurried over to the fire, spreading his chilled hands to warm them.

"Hance, before you get too comfortable, will you go down in the cellar and bring up a couple jars of blackberries for breakfast?"

"Sure, I will be glad to," he said, grinning at her and giving her a peck on the cheek as he passed. When he returned, he had the two jars of fruit and a pan of bright red apples. He set the pan of apples on the table so everyone could take what they wanted. Papa peeled and cored one for me. He peeled one side of another apple, picked up a small spoon, and went over and sat in Mamma's rocker.

Esther stood up and ran to Papa. Tugging at his pant leg, she said, "Apple, Papa, apple." Smiling, he picked her up, set her on his lap, and proceeded to scrape the peeled portion of the apple with the spoon and feed it to her.

Esther was only eighteen months old and Papa took no chances with her choking on a piece of apple.

Mamma set her bread starter on the sideboard where three large loaves of bread sat on cooling racks. Checking, she decided the bread was cool enough to store. She placed them in the metal breadbox in the cabinet. With kitchen chores finished, she walked over to the fire where Papa sat rocking Esther. Papa stood up and gave Mamma the rocker. She smiled lovingly at him as she accepted a kiss and Esther, and sat down in her rocker.

Suddenly, over the roar of the storm was a loud banging noise, "Clang! Squeak! Clap! Clap!" Papa stood up and headed for the door.

"What is it Hance?" Mamma asked.

"It must be the windmill. It sounds as if the chain has broken loose and the wind is whipping the blades back and forth. I will have to climb up and fasten it down or we won't have a windmill," he answered, as he reached for his coat and hat.

Mamma set Esther on the floor and rushed after him. "Hance, please don't go out there. What can you do in this storm? Let it go. It's too dangerous." Mamma sounded frightened. "You could be killed. That chain flipping around in the wind could knock you off or you could be decapitated with one of those blades. Wait until morning," she pleaded. "You could be struck by lightning in this storm."

Papa had his hat, coat, and boots on and was lighting the kerosene lantern.

"Gladys, I don't have a choice. If I let it go until morning, we may not have a windmill. Without a windmill, we wont have water to drink or to water the stock. Don't worry, I will be careful." Kissing her, he was out the door.

"You boys watch Esther," Mamma ordered as she hurriedly donned her coat, hat and boots. Picking up a second lantern, she lit it and dashed out after Papa.

I ran to the window and watched. I could see Papa climbing the ladder of the windmill. When lightning flashed, I could see the huge blades flopping wildly in the wind, and the loose chain hitting the metal framework. I was so frightened, I could scarcely breathe.

Mamma stood at the base of the windmill, holding her lantern high.

Anchoring his lantern, Papa watched the swinging chain. When it flipped close, he caught it. Papa was a very strong man, having worked with large animals and having done farm work all his life, but with the winds whipping the blades, it took all his strength to fasten the chain down to secure them.

Mamma stood waiting, the wind-driven rain whipping her long dress. When Papa reached the ground, I saw the two lanterns come together. Suddenly a great streak of lightning lit up the entire yard. I could see my parents embracing, seemingly oblivious to the wind and rain. I'm sure they were saying a prayer of thanks. Our world was once again set right.

## Chapter 10

# The Call Of The Bell

## Late Spring 1924

The chug, chug, chug of a gas-powered washing machine echoed across the yard where I was playing. Mamma was putting long poles under the sagging clotheslines. Snow-white sheets whipped and snapped in the warm spring breeze.

I was sitting on the edge of the back porch, watching a pair of robins building their nest in the tulip tree nearby.

Suddenly there was silence. Then I heard Mamma's exasperated voice, "Oh my land, not again! Ruth, run out to the barn and tell your father the washer has stopped again. This is the third time it has stopped today. I need him to see if he can find what is wrong with it or I will never get this laundry done. You will probably find him in the barnyard. He was going to be working with Old Merritt this morning. Now promise you won't go into the barnyard. Just call to him through the fence," Mamma ordered.

Old Merritt was Papa's prize bull. Papa had purchased the bull from a friend named Merritt, and decided to name the bull after his friend.

Papa with his prize bull, Old Merritt, and Shep

I ran as fast as I could, and by the time I reached the fence, I was breathless. I saw Papa leading Old Merritt from the barn. He had attached a twitch to the ring in the huge animal's nose. A twitch was a 2- or 3-foot heavy rod with a loop of rope or leather on the end, with a clasp that could be snapped onto the ring in the bull's nose. If he became difficult, a tug on the twitch straightened him out. I climbed up and sat on the top rail of the fence where I could watch Papa walk the magnificent animal around the yard. As he came near, Papa called out. "What are you doing here, Purtsy? Don't come down while I have Old Merritt out. He can be very dangerous."

" Mamma needs you to fix the washer. It won't work anymore."

"All right, you run tell her I will be in as soon as I put Old Merritt in the pasture".

Reluctantly, I climbed down from the fence and ran back to the house to deliver Papa's message, auburn curls bouncing as I ran. Mamma had gone in to fix dinner. I could smell ham frying as I burst into the kitchen. "Papa said he will be in as soon as he puts Old Merritt in the pasture." I said, breathlessly.

"Thank you Ruth. Now, will you take Esther outside and watch her while I finish dinner?"

Esther was two years old, two years younger than I. She had a pretty round face and fine auburn hair. Mamma would roll a curl on top but it didn't last. She said it was because Esther had been a sickly baby.

Taking my sister's hand, we went out to help Papa fix the washer. The washer was a wooden tub with a dasher inside. A belt went from the gears, under the tub, to a gas motor about eight or ten feet away. When the motor ran, the belt moved the gears, causing the washing action.

Papa worked and worked on the motor. It would start and run for a little while and stop. He would try something different. Suddenly the motor started, catching Papa's pant leg in the machinery, and he was pulled into the belt. He lay there with his leg twisted out of shape. I ran screaming, "Mamma! Mamma! Hurry! Papa is hurt! He is hurt bad!" I was crying and could hear Esther's terrified screams coming from the porch where I had left her.

Mamma moved her skillet to the back of the stove as she dashed past me. She ran, turned the motor off and started to try to help Papa but he stopped her. "Gladys, don't try. My leg is broken. Call Dr. Crampton."

Mamma said, "Ruth, go ring the dinner bell! John is working in the field; we will need his help."

I ran, climbed up on the stump below the bell, unhooked the bell rope, and rang it with all my strength. The sound of the big cast-iron bell could be heard echoing across the farm. John knew if the bell was rung and it wasn't dinnertime, there was something wrong. I could see him running across the field.

Esther and I sat on the platform next to Papa. We were both crying. I laid my head on Papa's chest and tried to hug him. Papa reached up and ran his hand thru my curls. "Don't cry, Purtsy. I am alright. When Dr. Crampton gets here, he will fix my leg like I fixed the dog's leg. Remember, when Shep's leg was broken, how you watched me put a splint on it? That is what the doctor will do to my leg. Now stop crying."

Mamma returned with a damp cloth to wipe off the beads of moisture that had formed on Papa's face.

When John arrived, he disconnected the belt and gently untangled it from Papa's leg. When the doctor arrived, they laid Papa out on the platform, and the doctor straightened the leg and splinted it. Mamma brought out crutches. With John's and the doctor's help, they got Papa up so he could walk into the house on crutches.

Being the only veterinarian for miles around, Papa wasn't down long. Farmers would call and he would tell them how to treat their animals over the phone. He couldn't charge for this because he didn't feel it was right if he hadn't done any work. People would bring their animals to him and he would walk out on crutches to examine and treat them. Then he started using the old buggy until his leg healed enough to drive the car.

I don't remember Mamma ever using that gasoline-powered washer after that.

## Chapter 11

# Shep Was My Best Friend

### Summer 1924

Mabel was not ready for a sister when I appeared on the scene, and it didn't take long for me to accept the fact that she didn't like me. I took too much of Mamma's time. I have often wondered if she associated my arrival with losing both of her grandmothers. Grandma Arrick died when I was still a baby, and Grandma Anderson two years later. They both doted over her and suddenly she had to share Mamma with a baby sister. I never dreamed that, as adults, we would become close friends.

In good weather, I could play outside, close to the house. Shep was my babysitter. She wouldn't let me go to the barn, the pasture, or the road. If I tried, she would bark and run back and forth in front of me until Mamma came to remind me of the rules.

When Mamma or Tracy went to the henhouse to gather eggs and feed the chickens, I would run along beside them. If I was careful, I was allowed to help gather the eggs. They would also let me go with them down the long lane to the road to get the mail.

Sometimes, when Esther wasn't feeling bad, Mamma would dress us in our Sunday clothes and we would go calling across the fields to Grandma Hartsock's. Living on a 240-acre farm, we had no close neighbors and no neighborhood children to play with. I understood that Mamma had to take care of the baby and that Esther was sick. I never resented that fact. As a result, however, I spent hours playing alone. I became very independent.

When Mabel wasn't in school, she played with the babies or her dolls. If she couldn't think of something else to do, she might play with me as long as I did as she said. She was bossy and I was independent, so that didn't work well. I would go to the window or out on the porch and watch for Papa. The minute his car stopped, I was there, dancing with joy. Papa would smile, pat my head, or pick me up and carry me back to the house. Only Papa made me feel wanted and loved.

Wayne was a healthy, happy baby, always laughing and smiling. When he got to the stage where he could crawl, Mamma would let me watch him while she took care of Esther or worked with Tracy. Esther's health was improving and we played together when Mabel was doing something else or was at school. When Mabel was home, she would talk Esther into doing something with her and I would be alone until Papa came home.

Papa's practice was taking him away more and more. Many days he was gone before I got up and not home before I was in bed

I liked playing with the boys, but they only tolerated me. They didn't want a four-year-old sister hanging around. I did learn a lot from Raymond, though not all of it good or true.

One day, I followed my brothers down to the pasture where John was watering the horses.

Raymond said, "Ruth, did you know if you put a hair from the horse's tail in the horse tank, it turns into a hair snake?"

"I don't believe you." I learned very young not to repeat anything Raymond said, do anything he did, or eat anything he offered me. Mamma said he tried to feed me a fish worm when I was a baby.

"Watch this if you don't believe me." Turning, he walked in back of the horse, pulled a hair from it's tail, and dropped it into the tank. I watched in amazement as the hair twisted and turned in the water like a snake.

Raymond was watching me as he said, "If you don't believe me, I dare you to take it out."

I put my hands behind me and stepped back one step. It acted like a snake, but I had seen him put the hair in the water.

"I told you it would change into a snake, but you wouldn't believe me. Now you can see for yourself. It will probably crawl out of the tank when it gets dark."

I don't know how many children I shared this knowledge with before I became old enough to realize that a soft breeze will move a hair floating on water.

On all farms there was an area where old equipment was placed out of sight of the house (a farm junkyard). I followed my brothers and watched Raymond reach into an old washing machine where bees had taken up residency. He pulled out a piece of honeycomb dripping with honey and started eating it. I loved honey and asked him to get me some.

"Get it yourself. You can reach in there just like I did."

"The bees will sting me. "They don't sting you," I pleaded.

Red walked back to the hive, reached in, and pulled out a piece of comb. Turning, he handed it to me with a mischievous smile on his face. I looked at the honeycomb in my hand. It didn't look like the one Raymond was eating. It wasn't dripping with honey. Looking past Raymond, I saw Arthur shaking his head. Handing the comb back to Raymond, I said, "This isn't like yours. I don't want it."

Raymond tossed it away and rolled on the ground laughing. He had given me a piece that was filled with baby bees.

Shep was tugging at my skirt, wanting to play. I looked down into her soulful eyes and thought to myself, Shep is my best friend. I let her lead me back to the porch, leaving Raymond to enjoy his bad joke.

Ruth, Mabel, and Esther

Raymond, Arthur, Mabel and Ruth

Raymond, Arthur, and Shep

## Chapter 12

# Going Calling

## Fall 1924

Three half-gallon buckets that had at one time held peanut butter or molasses stood open on the kitchen table. Mamma was putting an apple, a sandwich, and a large sugar cookie into each. Four bowls of oatmeal with a generous serving of fresh cream and a glass of milk stood waiting for the four of us. Mamma and Papa had eaten long before we were up. Esther was sitting in her highchair, finishing her breakfast.

Raymond came into the kitchen, his hair slicked down and his freckled face shining from having just been washed. Dropping his belt-bound books onto an empty chair, he headed for his place at the table. As he passed, he leaned over his dinner pail and sniffed, "Peanut butter and jelly again? Yuck!"

"Why Raymond! You know you like peanut butter and jelly. What would you rather have?"

Thinking for a second, he responded with a mischievous grin, "Fried chicken."

Mamma knew she was being teased but said seriously, "All right, when the weather gets cooler and I don't have to worry about it spoiling, I will fix fried chicken for you once in a while. Now you three hurry and finish your breakfast or you will be late for school."

Mamma took a washcloth from the hook over the washstand. Dipping the long-handled dipper into the water bucket, she ladled water into a basin. Wetting the cloth, she wiped three faces, kissing each as she went. "Hurry along now," she said, as she handed Raymond, Arthur and Mabel their lunch buckets and followed them out onto the porch. "You boys look after your sister now, and don't let her get hurt."

Our dog Shep had been waiting. She ran back and forth between the children. Her long hair was a mix of brown and black with a white chest and the tip of her long bushy tail. Her face was white with black ears and a black streak down the center separating her soulful eyes. Her coat was already getting thick in readiness for a cold Indiana winter. At the gate, Raymond stopped, gave the dog a hug, and ordered her back to the house. She stood a moment, her big sad eyes begging. "You can't go, Shep," Raymond said as sternly as he could.

"Here, Shep," Mamma called from the porch, where she still stood. Reluctantly, Shep headed back to the house, turning several times to see if maybe Raymond would change his mind and call.

I had just finished my oatmeal when Mamma returned to the kitchen. Mamma caught me as I started for the door. "Just a minute, young lady. You are not going anywhere until I wash your hands and face. Would you like to go calling on Grandma Hartsock this morning?" Grandma Hartsock was not related to us. She had been a good friend of Grandma Anderson and Papa had always called her Grandma.

"Yes, Mamma." I answered, as I jumped for joy. I knew there was always a treat at Grandma Hartsock's.

"All right, run and get the comb and brush so I can curl your hair. You have to look nice when we go calling."

I hated having my hair combed. It was very thick and curly. No matter how hard Mamma tried to be gentle, it pulled.

Mamma emptied the washbasin into the bucket that stood beside the washstand. Later, she or Papa would carry it out and pour it onto the flowers or empty it in the garden. Ladling clean water into the basin, Mamma turned and placed it on the table next to her chair and began to brush my hair. "Ouch! That hurts! Ouch!" I shouted as I tried to pull away.

"Stand still, Ruth! How do you expect me to get the tangles out if you keep squirming and fussing? Don't you want to look nice when we go calling?" At this point, I couldn't have cared less.

"But it hurts, Mama! You pull too hard," I complained.

"I'm sorry, Ruth, but your hair is so thick, it's hard to comb through the rat's nests."

"How did rats get in my hair?" I asked, reaching up to feel my head. "Are they still there?"

"Of course not," Mamma laughed, "That's just a silly expression grownups use to describe tangles in the hair."

Mamma dipped the celluloid comb into the basin and proceeded to wet my hair one section at a time, combing it tightly around her finger. She would comb the ends in and slide it off her finger with the comb, making a row of long, auburn curls that hung down over my shoulders.

Lifting Esther from her highchair where she had been playing and watching my torture, Mamma picked up a basket of goodies. No one went calling empty-handed.

"Ruth, run ahead and hold the screen door open for me, please. I have my hands full."

I let the door slam shut behind us. As we started on our way, we passed the garden, which looked pretty sad at this time of year except for the bright orange pumpkins just waiting to be gathered.

Mamma set her basket down on the other side of the split-rail fence and climbed over with Esther. I ignored the hand she offered and scrambled over after her. Walking through the corn stubble, we could see Grandma Hartsock's house in the distance. To a four-year-old, it seemed a long way off. I had a hard time keeping up with Mamma as we crossed the field.

When we finally reached the house, Mamma climbed up onto the porch, tapped on the screen door and called out, "Anybody home?"

From inside came a cheerful response. "Come on in, Gladys. I'm just sitting here, weaving. What a pleasant surprise! My land, how your girls have grown! Come here, Ruth. I think I might have something for you." Lifting the lid from a cut-glass candy dish, she held the dish out to me. I smiled at her as I chose the largest piece of taffy I could find. "Here's a piece of fudge for Esther. I'm afraid she might choke on taffy."

"What do you say, Ruth?" Mamma prodded.

"Thank you, Grandma."

She smiled as she lifted one of my curls, gently admiring it. "You have very pretty hair, Ruth. It's the same color as your father's." My smile thanked her.

Grandma's living room was neatly cluttered. There were huge spools of string stacked on the table and baskets of rag balls under the table. The huge loom took up the greatest part of the room. There were strings drawn tightly across the frame. Grandma was weaving rag strips through the strings with a large, handmade wooden needle. As she finished a row, it was pushed tightly against the previous row. When the multicolored rug was completed, the strings would be cut and tied, leaving a string fringe at each end.

"I brought you a little something, Grandma. Hance sent these pills for your baby chicks. He said you should dissolve 4 pills in a gallon of water and then fill the chicken waterers with it. I also brought you some cider apple butter, tomato preserves, and a jar of bread-and-butter pickles. The pickles are from a new recipe, so let me know if you like them as well as the old one." As she spoke, Mamma lifted the jars from her basket and set them on the table beside Grandma.

"My goodness, Gladys! You spoil me! I see you brought me another ball of rags. I certainly appreciate all these things. I have finished your rug," she said as she turned and lifted a rug from the stack behind her. "You may recognize your old blue dress and Hance's shirt in it."

Nothing was wasted on the farm. When clothes could no longer be mended, they were cut into quilt pieces or torn into narrow strips, sewn together and rolled into a ball. If they couldn't be used that way, they would be used as cleaning rags or stuffed into a huge flour sack and saved for the ragman.

Mamma reached into her apron pocket for money for the rug. Grandma stopped her. "Never you mind, dear. You don't owe me a penny. It gives me pleasure being able to give you something. You and Hance are so good to me. Hance never lets me pay him for taking care of my animals. It's the least I can do."

Mamma sat and visited while Esther and I played with empty string spools, until Esther began to fuss. "I'm sorry I can't stay any longer, Grandma, but Wayne will be getting hungry about now. I left him with the hired girl. Also, I can't be away from the phone too long. The hired girl doesn't know what to tell the customers when they call. Thank you so much for the rug, but you should let me pay you. I know you need the money. I'll send the boys over to bring in a good supply of wood for you." Mamma kissed Grandma's wrinkled cheek and Esther and I gave her big hugs as we started out the door.

"Now, you come back real soon," she called after us. "Remember me to your family."

Mamma waved as she hurried me down the steps toward home.

*Chapter 13*

# Making Soap

It was a beautiful Indian-summer day. The sky was as blue as a robin's egg. Puffy white clouds moved slowly through that sea of blue, changing shapes as they went. The smell of fall was in the air.

"Ruth," Mamma called, "I am going to show you how I make lye for soap. Then we will go to the woods to get sassafras roots for tea. Esther and Wayne are napping, so it's a good time to go." Mabel and the boys were at school.

Mamma handed me a basketful of cornhusks to carry. She carried a bucket of ashes from the stove in one hand, and a spade in the other. I was almost five, but I had to run to keep up with her as we walked across the yard to the shed. Inside the shed was a wooden box with a hole in one end near the bottom. The box sat on a low bench. Attached to the bench, below the hole in the box, was a trough tilting down to an old crock on the dirt floor.

Mamma lined the box with cornhusks and poured the bucket of wood ash on top. Picking up the bucket, she walked across to the horse-tank, filled it with water from the tank, and returned. I watched as she slowly poured the water over the ashes. "The water will slowly seep through the ashes and run into the crock", she explained. "But it won't be water then. It will have changed to lye. You must never touch lye. It would burn as bad as if you touched the hot stove. That is why we let it run into a crock instead of a bucket. It would eat right through a bucket. "In a few days, when the water has run thru the ashes, I will show you how I make soap. Would you like that?"

"Yes, but I don't like that soap. It hurts my hands and it stinks."

"Are you ready to go to the woods?" she asked?

I was always ready to go to the woods. I danced along beside her, swinging my basket. We sang "Jesus Loves Me" as we went. Mamma had a beautiful voice and had taught us many songs while she played the pump organ.

Walking across the field, Mamma said, "Nothing is prettier than the changing leaves in fall. Don't you think they are pretty, Ruth? No artist could paint them as you see them. Each tree has a different color. There is gold, yellow, red, green and brown. Which color do you like best Ruth?"

"I like the maple trees," I answered, "They have all the colors and every leaf is different. When the sun shines on the maple, it lights up. Do you think God likes the maple tree best and that's why he painted it the prettiest?"

Mamma smiled. "Well, maybe someone else likes the red and gold of the oak best. Maybe God thinks they are all equally beautiful. Only he knows, but we can have our favorites and God doesn't mind."

As we approached the woods, the pungent smell of the black walnut and hickory trees, along with the musty smell of rotting wood and leaves, filled our nostrils. I still love the fragrance of the woods.

"Ruth, can you tell me which tree is the sassafras?"

I walked into the thick woods, trying to avoid the brambles of the wild blackberry and the cockleburs. I went from tree to tree, sniffing the leaves as I went, until I came to a clump of small trees. "This one, this is the sassafras. I can tell cause it smells like sassafras tea."

Mamma was pleased. "You are right," she said, "See the leaves. They have three fingers. You like to play in the woods. It's important that you learn the trees and plants that are useful and safe. Some plants and shrubs are poison. Do you know what that plant over there is?" she said as she pointed to a low, red bush. I shook my head. "It is poison oak. It is green in the summer and turns red in the fall, so you can't go by the color. See, it has three leaves like poison ivy. Just remember, you stay away from any vine or bush with three leaves. I'll teach you a rhyme to help you remember; 'Leaves of three, let it be.' Can you remember that?"

I repeated the rhyme over and over as I watched. She placed her spade in the soft earth and dug up some of the young roots of the sassafras tree. She cut them off with the spade and placed them in my basket. When we had enough, she said, "There, that will be enough for the soap and tea for supper. We had better head back. Esther and Wayne will be awake."

Mamma carried the basket as we walked out of the woods. My feet sank deep in the fallen leaves and the years of mulch buildup. When we reached the edge of the woods, Mamma looked at her long dress and laughed. There were cockleburs all over her dress. My long cotton stockings and dress were also full of burs. We stopped and picked them off but I could feel little prickly bristles that broke off in my stockings. Mamma said, "When we get back to the house, you can change your stockings."

As we walked, we would stop to gather greens. She taught me which greens were good to eat and which were poison. "See this leaf," she said. "It looks like curly dock, but it has a red vein in it; it is poison." We picked curly dock, dandelion leaves, lamb's quarter, mustard, and whatever we came upon that Mamma said was edible. She placed them in the basket on top of the sassafras.

I was dragging behind as we headed home, until I saw Papa getting out of his car in front of the house. I took off on the run, oblivious to the prickly bristles in my stockings, shouting, "Papa! Papa!"

"Well, here's my Purtsy girl. What have you been doing?" he said as he leaned over and picked me up for my hug.

"Mamma and I made lye and dug sassafras and picked greens and we got burs all over us!"

"I can tell. I feel them in your clothes. You had better go change them," he said as he set me down and kissed Mamma.

It was two weeks before Mamma decided it was a good day to make the soap. Papa and John had hung the huge cast-iron kettle on a tripod over a fire pit. They had stacked wood nearby and set the fire under the kettle ready for lighting. After breakfast, Mamma put a coat on Esther and said, "Ruth, run get your coat. It's chilly out. Esther, you can't stay out very long, but I think you need some fresh air."

Esther and I were waiting at the edge of the porch when

Mamma came out with buckets of waste fat. We followed her out across the dead grass of the lawn to the fire pit, where she set the buckets of fat on the ground and lit the fire under the kettle. "Ruth, why don't you girls go over to the fence and see the sheep while I move the lye from the shed?"

That sounded great to me. I much preferred animals to making soap. Esther and I ran to the fence and watched as the sheep came running to us, hoping for food. We stretched our arms through the fence to pet as many as we could reach. I recognized one of the spring lambs that I had fed with a bottle when her mother died. The bigger sheep were crowding her out.

I was halfway over the fence when I heard, "Winona Ruth, get down off that fence. You are supposed to be watching your sister! Why are you such a tomboy? You two can come back here now. I am ready to make the soap."

Reluctantly, I took my sister's hand and hurried back to watch Mamma pour the lye into the kettle. The fire was blazing by now. When the lye was boiling, Mamma measured out the fat she had saved for this purpose, dropped it into the kettle, and stirred it with a long, flat, wooden paddle.

On the farm, nothing was wasted. Any fat could be used for soap. Fat from butchering cows or sheep was rendered out and saved, as well as waste fat from cooking. Mamma preferred the fat from sheep. She thought it was easier on the hands and, unlike lard, it couldn't be used for cooking. Making soap was a slow process. It had to be stirred constantly.

I heard the door of the house slam shut and saw Tracy coming toward us carrying a bucket and several large baking pans. "I came to relieve you. I know that stirring gets pretty tiring. Wayne is fussing and hungry, and only you can take care of that. I brought the sassafras tea and can take over for you here.

Mamma smiled, "Thank you Tracy. I think Esther has been out here long enough too. If I am not back by the time the soap thickens, send Ruth for me. I will feed Wayne and Esther, get them down for their naps, and be back in time to relieve you."

I watched Tracy stir the smelly, boiling mixture. I can still smell that stench of mutton fat.

By the time Mamma returned, the soap was thickening, and Mamma added the strong sassafras tea to the kettle. This was supposed to give the soap a fragrance, but to me it still stank. Several pans had been laid out on the end of the nearby butchering table. With long-handled dippers, Mamma and Tracy ladled the hot mixture into the pans to cool. As it cooled, it hardened, and would be cut into rectangular pieces. The soap cleaned clothes, but it was rough on hands.

# Chapter 14

# Wash Day

## December 1924

It was still dark outside when Papa slipped out of bed, dressed, and went into the kitchen. He quietly shut the door behind him. Lifting the chimney of the wall-hung kerosene lamp, he struck a kitchen match, lit the wick, replaced the chimney, and adjusted the flame. The cold room took on a soft glow.

The fire in the big, potbellied, wood-burning stove that heated our home had been banked the night before. Taking the long poker from its hook on the side of the stove, he stirred the coals and tossed in corncobs or kindling wood. When these caught fire, large logs were laid in and soon a hot fire was blazing.

Papa then went to the kitchen and started a fire in the cook stove. He placed a large copper boiler over the firebox of the stove, and carried in buckets of water to fill the boiler and the stove's reservoir.

Copper wash boiler

By the time the fires were going well, Mamma came out of the bedroom with our baby. After she changed and dressed him, she set him on a quilt on the floor. She laid dining chairs on their sides and put them around Wayne, creating a pen so he couldn't get near the heating stove.

"John must be here," Papa said, "I see a light in the barn. I'll bring in some more wood and then go help him with the milking."

The sound of stomping feet was followed by the door opening, and Tracy, our hired girl, slipped in, quickly closing the door to keep the cold out.

"Good morning, Tracy. Did you have a good weekend?" Papa asked, as he picked up four large milk pails and started for the door.

"Yes, thank you," she answered. "I hope you don't have many calls today, Dr. Anderson. It's freezing out there and snowing hard."

The teakettle was beginning to sing. Mamma and Tracy exchanged greetings and together they started breakfast.

When Papa and John finished their chores, they brought the warm milk to the springhouse where it was strained into five-gallon milk cans. These were placed in the center of the round tub of ice-cold water to chill. When chilled, they would be carried down the long drive to the edge of the road to be picked up by the milkman, who took them to a place where the milk was bottled and delivered to homes in town and to stores. At the end of the month, Papa would receive a check.

John and Papa removed their knee boots before entering the house. The aroma of coffee filled the kitchen.

"How's my boy?" Papa asked, as he picked Wayne up and placed him in his highchair. By the time the men had washed, breakfast was on the table. Farmers ate very well. There was always a big breakfast because they had already done two to three hours of work. Almost everything on the table had been raised by us or made from what we had raised. Papa had just butchered a hog, so we had fresh sausage, eggs, homemade bread, fresh churned butter, wild blackberry jam, canned fruit, steaming oatmeal, and thick, fresh cream. No one touched a utensil until Papa had thanked God for our blessings.

After discussing what was going on in the little towns of Pittsburgh and nearby Delphi, Papa would tell John what he wanted done. "I'd like for you to hitch up the team and bring in the rest of the wood from the tree we cut up last week. We should get it in before the snow gets too deep. All the signs show we are in for a long, cold winter. If I get back from my calls in time, I will help you. Before I leave,

I'll help you fill the wood-boxes, and then I had better run." Papa said, as he pushed back his chair.

As John shoved his chair back he said, "Don't you worry about the wood-boxes, Hance. I'll take care of them. You better get going. That snow is really coming down. You don't want to get stuck on some country road."

Papa was putting on his coat and his hat with the earflaps pulled down. "You are probably right John," he said. Kissing Mamma goodbye, he went out to the mudroom, put on his boots, and headed for the car, carrying a handful of medicine bottles to place in his bag.

While Tracy cleared the table and set it for the children, Mamma went to the stair door and called, "It is time to get up, children. Breakfast is ready. It is washday, so gather up your dirty clothes and your bottom sheets. Put your clean long underwear on. It's really cold out." As she closed the door to the stair, a gush of cold air was forced into the room. Bedrooms were never heated. On washdays, the bottom sheet was washed and the top sheet was used as a bottom sheet. After all, your body only touched one side of it.

I hated getting out of a warm bed and dressing in a cold room, so I would place my clothes behind the stove and they would be warm. I dashed down the stairs and slipped behind the stove. While I dressed, Mamma was dressing Esther. "Come on girls, lets get washed up for breakfast," she said, as she ushered us over to the washbasin that set on the washstand beside the kitchen door. She ladled a dipper of water from the water bucket into the basin, along with a dipper of hot water from the reservoir at the end of the stove. We were each washed with the washcloth she kept on the towel rack on the end of the washstand, and then sent to the table.

Mamma lifted Esther into her highchair. I was five; I didn't need help. The large pan of oatmeal had been placed on the back of the stove to keep warm. Oatmeal was spooned into two ironstone bowls and placed in front of us. Mamma put sugar on the cereal in each bowl and started to pour cream from the pitcher onto mine.

"No, I want to do it," I begged. "You pour too much and I can't see the sugar."

"All right, but if you spill it, young lady, you are in trouble. I am too busy to have to clean up messes," she said, as she poured it on Esther's and poured each of us a glass of milk.

Two large galvanized tubs had been set up on low benches at the end of the kitchen. At the right of the tubs stood a rocker-washer. A hand-crank wringer was set on the tub next to the washer. Tracy had been carrying buckets of water from the pump on the back porch to fill the tubs about half full. She dipped enough hot water from the boiler on the stove to warm the water in the tubs. She returned to the pump for more water to replace what she had removed from the boiler.

Piles of clothes that had been sorted according to color and degree of soil were stacked nearby. Papa's work clothes, which were usually very stained and soiled, had been put in a separate tub of warm soapy water to soak.

One by one, the children wandered in, carrying their dirty clothes and placing them in the appropriate piles. While Mamma made their lunches, they washed and helped themselves to the oatmeal, a glass of milk, and fruit.

Mamma hurriedly curled Mabel's hair and pulled clean mittens through the sleeves of the children's coats. (Mittens were fastened together with a heavy cord and laced through the coat sleeves. When you removed your coat the mittens stayed in the coat. This way, there was never a reason for losing your mittens.) "Run get your galoshes Mabel. Do you boys have yours? It is snowing hard and I don't want you catching cold from sitting in school all day with wet feet."

"We have them on," Raymond answered. "Hurry up, Mabel! Why do we always have to wait for her? She's so pokey, we will miss the hack!"

"Be nice, Raymond. You boys run ahead. She will catch up," Mamma said, as she buckled the last buckle on Mabel's galoshes, pulled a cap with an attached scarf onto her head, and helped her into her coat. Handing Mabel her dinner pail, she kissed her and said, "Run now, and shut the door behind you so you don't let the cold air in."

We always had beans for supper on washday. A pot of beans had been soaking all night. Mamma lifted the beans out of the water into a three-legged cast iron pot, covered them with fresh water, and seasoned them with salt, pepper and either a chunk of ham or bacon drippings. Taking the lifter from its hook, she lifted the stove lid from one of the eyes over the back of the oven, and the cast-iron kettle fit perfectly into the eye. The beans would cook slowly all day.

Tracy had shaved a bar of lye soap and dropped it into the boiler. Picking up the clothes stick, which had been made from a broom handle, she stirred the water to dissolve the soap. Dipping a bucket into the boiler she carefully lifted out a bucket of hot, soapy water and poured it into the washer.

Gathering up the sheets, pillowcases, white shirts and

towels, one by one she placed them in the boiler, stirring them around with the clothes stick.

Taking the shaker from its hook at the end of the stove, she placed it over a square knob below the firebox and shook it back and forth, shaking the ashes down into the ash box below. Carefully opening the door of the firebox, so as not to allow live coals to drop out onto the floor, she added more wood to the fire.

Our washer was a concave copper tub, set in a wooden frame that was supported by four legs. The rocker cradle looked like a wooden washboard curved to fit the tub. There was a triangular framework on each side of the rocker scrubber, through which ran a round rod that extended on each side. These extensions slid into brackets on each side of the tub, allowing the scrubber to rock back and forth and move up or down according to the size of the load. When the clothes were clean, the cradle was hung on the end of the washer and the clothes put through the wringer into the first tub of rinse water.

When the first batch of white clothes had boiled a few minutes, Mamma removed the lid of the boiler. She stepped back from the burst of steam that was released. With the clothes stick, she carefully lifted the steaming clothes from the boiler into a large pan. Carrying it to the washer, she dumped it in. Picking up a bucket, she returned to the boiler, lifted out a bucket of hot suds and poured it into the washer. She cooled it down with cold water. Another bucket of cold water and more soap was added to the boiler. The second batch of white clothes was then added, stirred, and covered to boil.

Mamma made starch while Tracy washed the first batch. All shirts, dresses, tablecloths, and pillow cases had to be starched. She examined the colored clothes, separating the light colored from the dark colored. The badly soiled were put to soak while the whites were being washed.

Tracy placed the rocker in its brackets over the clothes in the washer, rocking it back and forth, scrubbing them clean. The clothes had to be checked to be sure all spots had come out; if not, they would be rubbed with lye soap and scrubbed on the scrub board. Satisfied that they were clean, she fed the clothes through the hand wringer into the first tub of rinse water. The wringer was moved to the second tub and the clothes fed through, into the second rinse. It would be moved again to the other side of second tub allowing the clothes to fall into the clothes basket after the final rinse. After the second rinse, those items that needed starch were set aside.

Tracy had finished rinsing the first batch. Putting on her coat, hat and boots, she grabbed up the clothespins, picked up a loaded basket of clothes, and headed outside to hang them. When the icy air hit the warm wet clothes, you could see steam rise from the basket.

The second batch was taken from the boiler and the process was repeated. Diapers were the last load to go into the boiler. When they were boiled, Mamma and Tracy carried the boiler out back and dumped it. Fresh water was put in the boiler to heat.

Mamma had just finished washing the second load of whites, when Tracy returned from the line, her face and hands beet-red. She was happy to put her cold hands in the warm rinse water while Mamma took out the last load of whites from the boiler.

After all the white clothes had been washed, Tracy and Mamma carried the huge tubs out the back door and emptied them away from the walkway. The tubs were returned and refilled with water from the pump.

It was now time for the colored clothes. Mamma had put the badly soiled clothes to soak. She wrung them out one at a time. Each item was checked and lye soap rubbed into any spot or stain. Turning it over, it would be scrubbed on the scrub board until the spots were removed or Mamma decided the stain was there to stay. She then put them into the washer and rocked them back and forth until clean. Stockings had to be turned between the first and second rinses to be sure that all the sand and grass had been washed out. This was my job.

While Tracy washed the clothes, Mamma checked Papa's work clothes that had been soaking. Sudsing them up and down in the soaking water, she wrung them out, and put them in clean wash water. Placing the scrub board into the water she would lift one piece of clothing at a time, place it onto the scrub board and rub lye soap into the stains. Turning the garment over, she scrubbed it vigorously on the scrub board. Dipping the garment back into the water, she sudsed it up and down, repeating this process until the stain came out or she was satisfied that it never wood. Wringing them out, she placed them in the washer and washed them again.

When all the clothes had been washed, a bucket was placed under the washer. It was then drained and the water from the washer was carried, a bucket at a time, and thrown into the snow. Mamma was careful not to throw it in the path where someone would slip on the ice that would form.

Mamma worked side by side with Tracy, stopping only to answer the phone or take care of the baby. She had placed me in charge of entertaining Esther and Wayne. I was to see that they stayed on the other side of the kitchen, away from danger.

Together, Mamma and Tracy would carry the big tubs of rinse water outside, dump them, and carry buckets of clean water into the house to refill them. Before they went out to the line together, Mamma would check the baby's diaper, change it if necessary, and remind me to take good care of Esther and Wayne. Mamma would start dinner while Tracy finished hanging the clothes. She knew John would be listening for the dinner bell.

The phone rang. It was Papa calling to see if he had had any calls. "I won't be home for dinner Gladys, I am still at the Brown's. I am not quite finished here. Henry Johnson saw me drive by his place. He drove over here to see if I could stop by. He has a cow in trouble. Mrs. Brown has fixed dinner for me. As soon as I finish here, I will run by the Johnsons'. I will call you before I leave there. It's hard to say when I will be home, but you know where to reach me."

"Alright, Hance, but do be careful. The roads are slick." she cautioned. "You don't have any more calls that can't wait until tomorrow."

Mamma went into the springhouse and brought back a pan of potatoes and a home-cured ham. She went into the pantry and came out with a jar of vegetables and a jar of fruit. By the time Tracy returned from the line, Mamma had potatoes frying in one large cast-iron skillet and generous slices of ham in another. The jar of peas had been opened, placed in a pan and were simmering on the back of the stove.

"Tracy, will you keep an eye on dinner while I take care of the baby?"

"Sure," she answered, as she started setting the table. "It has stopped snowing and the sun has come out, but it is really cold out there."

Mamma fed Wayne, changed his diaper, placed him in the little crib near the stove, and went back to the kitchen. Tracy stepped out the door and rang the bell while Mamma took up the food and got Esther up in her highchair. The heat of the room had melted the heavy coat of ice from the upper part of the windows, leaving a thick build-up of ice along the lower two inches of the glass. I saw John driving Papa's team of Percherons. They were pulling a big sled filled with wood up to the woodpile. Unhooking the horses, he led them to the horse tank in the barnyard. He had to break the ice in the tank so they could drink. After taking them into the barn and removing their harness, he came into the kitchen, washed in the basin on the washstand, and joined us for dinner. Papa was still on calls.

After dinner, John helped Tracy empty the tubs and washer. The tubs were hung on the wall of the mudroom; the washer was moved up against the wall of the kitchen, out of the way. Tracy mopped up the oak plank floor and hung the rag mop on a hook outside the door.

Mamma put Esther down for her nap while Tracy set up wooden clothes racks around the heating stove. A line had been strung behind the cook stove. "Ruth, if you put on your boots, coat and hat, you can go out and watch John unload the wood and watch for Papa while Tracy and I bring in the clothes that are dry." I hated being housebound and ran to obey.

When I stepped outside, wrapped up like a mummy, I ran out to the woodpile. Snow covered the wood like a fluffy white blanket. The snow had set on the bare trees and shrubs, creating a fairyland. The dead plants that had been left in the garden were covered with snow, no longer looking dry and ugly. Looking back at the house, I saw a row of huge long icicles hanging from the edge of the roof.

The clothes on the line were frozen stiff. I followed as Tracy carried them into the house. It was too cold for me outside. I removed my coat, hat, and boots near the door. Mamma and Tracy were hanging the frozen clothes on the racks and the line behind the cook stove. When they ran out of space, they pulled the bentwood kitchen chairs up to the stoves and laid clothes over them. They were turned frequently so that the damp side was always next to the fire. As the clothes dried, they were folded and replaced with the next load.

The clothes that needed ironing were rolled up while they were still damp, wrapped in a piece of old sheet, and placed in a clothes basket. Most everything was ironed: sheets, tea towels, shirts, slips, pants, tablecloths, and napkins. About the only clothing that didn't get ironed was our long underwear, socks and Wayne's diapers.

Tomorrow, Mamma would iron. We had several flatirons that were placed on the cook stove to heat. She would set up the ironing board and place a folded newspaper on the end of the board, along with a rack for the iron. Mamma would place a handle on one of the irons and pull up a little knob, locking it safely to the iron. To check to see if it was warm enough, she lifted the iron, licked a finger and touched it quickly to the bottom of the iron, causing a sizzling sound. When the iron cooled down, she would place it back on the stove and pick up another iron. If an iron had set on the stove for some time and she thought it might be too hot, she would run it across the newspaper. If it scorched the paper, it was set back on the stove, away from the heat, and another was checked.

The dampness from the steaming clothes hung heavy in the air, causing the windows to steam over. The fresh clean smell of the clothes mingled with the smell of cooking beans.

After washing up the dishes from dinner, Tracy went upstairs to make the beds. Mamma started preparing supper. "Ruth, why don't you watch for Mabel and the boys?" she asked.

I ran to the window and waited. The window kept fogging up and I would wipe it with my sleeve so I could see. Finally the hack stopped at the end of our long lane. The minute the door opened, Raymond jumped out, not bothering with the steps or looking back. Arthur and Mabel stepped down and followed him on the run.

"They're coming! They're coming!" I shouted.

"Hush, Ruth, you will wake the baby." Mamma's warning came too late. Wayne sat up smiling at his sister and brothers as they rushed in, pink cheeked and breathless. Esther came running out of the bedroom. Mamma sent her back to close the door. Dinner pails and books were set noisily on the table.

Mable rushed up to Mamma and burst out, "Mamma! Mamma! Raymond was naughty in school and the teacher made him sit on a chair in the corner."

"Tattletale, Tattletale, hanging on a bull's tale," Raymond snarled.

"Raymond, that's enough. What did you do that the teacher made you sit in the corner?"

"I didn't do anything. I just told Sally Higgins there was a bug on her back and she started screaming and jumping around. I guess when she started jumping around the bug jumped off 'cause the teacher couldn't find it and I had to sit in the corner. I always get blamed." Raymond grinned as he and Arthur exchanged knowing glances. Being in a one-room school had its disadvantages.

"Well, you children run change your clothes. You boys will have to hurry or it will be too dark to find the eggs. The wood-boxes need filling too. Mabel, when you get your clothes changed, I want you and Ruth to wash your hands and set the table."

Raymond and Arthur headed for the stairs. Arthur whispered, "What's going to happen when she finds the dead mouse in her desk?" We could hear giggling as they went up the stairs.

Mamma was stirring something in her crockery bowl. "What are you making?" I asked.

"Layover to catch a meddler," she answered, smiling. I didn't know what she meant by that, but I knew when she said it, she was fixing something good.

"I know what it is! It's soda cake!"

"How did you guess?" she asked.

"'Cause you always have beans and Soda Cake on washday." Soda cake was a delicious spice cake that was served warm and needed no frosting.

Mamma opened the oven, put her hand in to check the temperature, and, seeming satisfied, she placed the cake in the middle of the oven, closed the oven door, adjusted the damper, and added one stick of wood to the fire.

Arthur came in with the eggs and Raymond with a load of wood. They both went out again for more wood. I saw John carrying the milk into the spring house.

We finished supper and Papa still wasn't home. No matter what time he came in, Mamma would be up waiting for him, keeping the fire going and his supper warm.

# Chapter 15

## Aunt Mae

It was a crisp fall morning. Breakfast was over. Mabel, Raymond and Arthur were in school. Papa was putting on his heavy coat and gloves.

"Gladys, I think I will go over to Aunt Mae's before I get a lot of calls. I want to check on that cow I treated and drop off some medicine for their chickens. While I am there, I will check to be sure Floyd and George are ready to butcher hogs tomorrow. I will be back soon. I need to set things up so I will be ready when they get here in the morning."

"Can I go? Can I go? I want to see Aunt Mae," I shouted, jumping up and down.

Papa smiled down at me. "If it's okay with your mother, I guess you can come, Purtsy."

"Go ahead Ruth. I could use some peace and quiet around here, but remember you are not to touch anything at Aunt Mae's house and it isn't polite to ask for anything. Will you remember?"

"Yes," I replied, but my mind was going a mile a minute. I knew Aunt Mae would give me a glass of milk and a cookie without my asking. Papa helped me on with my coat and hat, kissed Mamma goodbye, and we were out the door.

Aunt Mae's farm was about a mile from ours, across the fields and up the road. She treated Papa like one of her boys, and he, being an only child, spent as much time with her and her family as he could. Aunt Mae had nine children, Stella, Myrtle, Mary, George, Floyd, John, Alfred, Harry and Bob. Papa and her children grew up together like sisters and brothers. This bond of love and friendship lasted throughout their lives.

Mamma tried to explain our relationship, but it was complicated. Papa's grandfather and their father were half-brothers. From here, Mamma would get into talking about half second-cousins once or twice removed, and no one could follow her. It didn't really make any difference. We felt like close relatives.

Papa's car rattled along the gravel road, leaving a dust trail behind. When we reached the lane that turned into Aunt Mae's place, Papa honked his horn. They knew his horn, and as we drove up the long tree-shaded lane, I could see their big, white, two-storied house with a porch that spanned the entire front. Papa drove to the rear of the house before stopping. George stepped out of the barn where he had been working and hurried over to greet us. I was already halfway to the house when I saw Aunt Mae open the door and call out to us.

"Hance, such a nice surprise. Ruth, come over here and let me look at you. My land, you are growing like a weed. Turn around and let me see your beautiful curls." She picked one curl up and let it bounce down my back. "If they get any longer, you will be sitting on them. You are so lucky to have thick curly hair." I thanked her as I was taught, but I wanted to tell her how I hated my thick hair. It was torture every morning when Mamma brushed and combed it to get the tangles out. Then I had to stand still while she wound it around her finger into long curls that fell to my waist.

"You boys come on in. I just made a pot of coffee," she called out. Come on in, Ruth. Myrtle is in the kitchen."

"I'll be in as soon as I take a look at that cow, Aunt Mae. I brought your chicken medicine," Papa said as he handed a bottle of pills to George and the two of them headed to the barn.

As we entered the kitchen, we could hear Papa and George laughing. I knew one of them had told a funny story. Myrtle was in the kitchen, taking cookies from the oven. She smiled as she watched me eye the cookies. She knew I wouldn't dare ask for one. It took her such a long time to set the hot cookies on cooling racks. She walked to the cupboard and set out four coffee cups and a glass. I tried not to look at the cookies, but my gaze kept returning.

Papa and George came in, still chuckling. Myrtle greeted them, coffee pot in hand. "Sit down, Hance. I just took these cookies out of the oven. Perfect timing. Ruth, would you like a glass of milk and a cookie?"

I looked at Papa. Did I dare say yes or would that be asking for something?

Papa grinned and answered for me, "She has just been waiting for you to offer. She has a sweet tooth."

"Thank you," I said as I took the milk and cookies that Myrtle put before me.

Myrtle was older than Floyd and George. She was a trained nurse and had never married. George didn't marry until he was much older. The Andersons were soft-spoken, gentle people and were a very close family. The boys liked to play tricks on each other, like the time John put a snake in the dynamite box. They used dynamite to remove tree stumps. Knowing how Alfred hated snakes, John asked him to get a couple of sticks of dynamite. The rest of the boys stood and watched as Al opened the box. He started to put his hand in and saw the snake. He slammed the lid shut and jumped back, not stopping to see that it was a harmless snake; however, he did see his brothers bent over in laughter, and took out after John who was already halfway across the field.

By the time we all finished our treat, George and Papa had made plans for butchering the next day. "I was just going over to Floyd's place to help him mend a fence. I know he is planning on helping us, but if there are any changes in his plans, I'll let you know. It will depend on Meryl. He may not feel he can leave her. Her time is coming close."

Grownups didn't speak of pregnancy in front of children. I wouldn't have known what they were talking about if they had. I didn't even make a connection when our babies were born. All I knew was, the doctor came to our house with his black bag, and when I awakened in the next morning, I had a new baby brother in the house.

"Well, if Meryl isn't feeling well, he won't want to leave her. You and I will go ahead as planned. John will be there to help us." Papa thanked everyone and ushered me out ahead of him. "We had better run. Gladys is going to think I got lost."

"Say hello to Gladys and the family," Myrtle called after us.

When we reached home, Mamma was putting three large loaves of bread in the oven. "Well Gladys, everything is set for tomorrow. The boys will be here bright and early."

"That is good," she answered. "I hope you don't get any urgent calls in the morning."

"Well, if I do, I know the boys will go ahead and take care of things for me. John will be here to help. I'll just have to make it up to them later. They understand that I can't let an animal die while I butcher a hog. Hopefully there will be no calls that can't wait."

"I see the wood-box needs filling. Is there anything else you need me to do before I go out to set things up for tomorrow?"

"I can't think of anything right now, dear. I am glad Tracy will be here to help me tomorrow."

"Mamma, can I go help Papa set things up?"

"Ask your father. You might get in his way," she answered.

Papa smiled down at me. "I guess you can come, Purtsy, but you will have to be a good girl and mind."

After filling the wood-box, Papa and I went to the barn. He gathered up ropes and pulleys, which he carried to the butchering table. This was a long table made of hickory wood planks, slightly lower at one end to allow for drainage. It had stood in our side yard near the barnyard fence for years. At the lower end of the table was a tall wooden frame with a heavy beam across the top. Papa rigged the ropes and pulleys on the cross bar, and as he did so, he explained that they would use the ropes and pulleys to lift the huge hog onto the table.

A large washtub was placed at the end of the table under

the framework. Papa pulled a small horse-watering tank from beneath the table, turned it upright and set it next to the tub.

I heard the clop, clop of horses hooves and, looking up, I saw John, our hired man, coming from the woods with Papa's powerful team of horses pulling a wagon full of wood. Their heavy winter coat hid the beauty of their rippling muscles. Their breath made puffs of steam in the crisp air. "Stand back Ruth. John is going to bring the horses in close and unload some wood here."

He and John worked together as they unloaded the wood. When Papa was satisfied that we had enough, he said, "John, you can put the rest of the wood up at the house."

"Okay, Hance. When I have finished, I will be back to help you hang the rendering kettle."

"Good. In the meantime, I will fetch some water and rinse it out." I watched John as he turned the team and headed away from us.

The rendering kettle was a huge cast-iron kettle, approximately three feet across, used for rendering lard. Mamma also used this kettle when she made soap.

Papa walked over to the fence and lifted a bucket off the top of a fence post. Our windmill pumped water through pipes to the house as well as the barn and the horse tank. Papa filled the bucket with water from the pipe that fed the horse tank. The heavy kettle had been leaned against a tree so that water wouldn't collect in it. Papa set the kettle upright, washed and rinsed it.

A heavy iron framework stood about ten feet from the end of the table. Under the framework were the remains of an old fire, circled with rocks. A heavy iron chain hung from the center of the frame. A large iron hook was fastened through the chain. Papa placed a pile of corncobs and small pieces of wood in the center of the ring of rocks. He then piled larger pieces on top until he had what would be a large hot fire under the kettle. He would be up before daylight to fill the kettle with water and get the fire going. The water had to be near boiling.

I saw John coming across the yard. "Hance, Gladys said dinner is ready and you have some calls. I can finish up anything here if you haven't finished."

"The only thing left to do is hang the kettle. Lets do that now and go eat."

The two men lifted the heavy kettle and placed its handle on the hook above the fire that had been laid.

"Purtsy, would you like to ride one of the horses over to the barn?" Papa lifted me up on the back of one of the horses, keeping one hand securely around my leg. Sitting on the back of that great horse was like sitting on a tabletop, high off the ground.

When we reached the barn, Papa lifted me down and said to John, "I'll see you at the house as soon as you get the horses taken care of." As we headed for the house, I could see Mamma step out the back door onto the porch. "Hance, Tom O'Farrell just called. He has a horse with colic. I told him you would be there as soon as you had eaten dinner. You have a couple other calls but I told them you couldn't come until you had finished at Tom's."

Chapter 16

# Butchering Day

I was awakened by Mamma calling up the stairs, "Mabel, you had better get up or you will miss the hack." I was glad I didn't have to go to school. I wanted to watch Papa butcher the hogs.

Slipping out of my warm bed, I ran across the cold floor to the window. The grass and the roof of the barn were white with frost. A fire was blazing under the big kettle of water, sending up a cloud of steam into the frosty air.

George and Floyd had just arrived with their hog and were talking to Papa and John. The pleasant sound of their laughter carried through the cold fall air. I knew I was missing something. I slipped into my long underwear and, dressing as quickly as I could, I ran down stairs, grabbed my coat from the hall-tree, and headed for the door.

"Winona Ruth, where do you think you're going? You haven't washed or eaten your breakfast."

"But Papa said I could watch him butcher the hog."

"You can go out after breakfast and after Papa has shot the hogs. You don't want to watch that, do you?"

"Yes I do. Raymond and Arthur are out there; they get to watch."

"That's different. They are boys."

"Why is it different? Boys get to do anything they want and girls don't get to do anything fun. I wish I was a boy."

"Ruth, stop complaining and get washed for breakfast," Mamma ordered.

I hurried through breakfast, washed, and ran to the window to be sure I wasn't missing anything. Papa was holding his revolver. The sun shone on its long silver barrel. Suddenly, two loud cracks rang out. I knew the hogs had been shot.

"Can I go now ?"

"We will both go, but I need you to help carry things."

Mamma had just finished curling Mabel's hair. Everyone admired Mabel's beautiful red hair. It was curlier than mine, but much thinner, so it didn't tangle as badly. She never seemed to mind having it brushed and curled.

Mamma handed Mabel her dinner bucket and said, "You had better hurry. The boys are already down at the end of the lane."

"Tracy, would you keep an eye on Esther and Wayne? I am taking Ruth with me. If you need, me just call."

"Don't worry, Gladys. I will take care of things here."

Mamma handed me a bag of cloths. She picked up two crocks and set them in a nest of large dishpans. "Ruth, you can hold the door for me." Together we crossed the yard to the butchering table.

By the time we got there, Papa had prepared a fire under the giant iron kettle. A huge black and white hog had been hoisted by its hind legs over a tub. Its throat had been cut to allow the blood to drain out. The second hog was hanging from a rope that had been thrown over a large limb of a nearby hickory tree.

George and John were carrying buckets of steaming water from the kettle and pouring it into a large metal tank. The empty kettle was then refilled with cold water. Mamma put more wood on the fire, as needed, to keep it going. A second kettle was hanging from a wrought-iron hook connected to a rod that allowed the kettle to be swung over a fire pit that had been filled with firewood. Mamma lit this fire, allowing it to burn to hot coals.

Floyd and Papa manipulated the ropes to carry the hog over the steaming tank as Papa guided it. They lowered the hog into the hot water. It was then hoisted up and onto the table and they began scraping off the hair.

Papa had placed rocks in the fire to heat. With heavy iron tongs, he carried some of them to the water tank. One by one he dropped them, spitting and hissing as they hit the water. This would be repeated periodically.

"Why did you do that?" I asked.

"That keeps the water from cooling off too much. We will be lowering the hog into it again. The hot water helps loosen the hair. We want to take off all the hair."

The men joked and laughed as they worked from both sides of the table, scraping the hair off with dull knives so as not to cut into the skin of the hog. When they finished one side, the hog was again lowered into the hot water, and then back onto the table and the other side was scraped clean. A bucket of clean hot water was carried from the kettle, and spots where the hair remained were scalded and scraped until the skin shone pink and clean.

The hog was washed with cold water and the head

removed. It was again raised, and the table scrubbed down. The washtub at the end of the table was removed and an empty one placed under the hog. With a razor-sharp knife, Papa carefully slit open the belly of the hog from neck to crotch, allowing the entrails to drop into the tub.

The liver, from which the gallbladder had been carefully removed, was placed in one of the pans along with the heart and kidneys and covered with cold water. We would have liver for supper tonight. It was always best really fresh.

Methodically, the three men skinned the hog. The skin, thick with fat, was cubed and tossed into a pan, along with the fat that was cut away from the meat. When a pan was filled, it was carried over and dumped into the huge wrought-iron rendering kettle where Mamma was waiting. The fat sizzled and snapped when it hit the hot iron kettle.

Papa used knives, saws and a hand ax to cut up a hog. All pieces of scrap meat were tossed into one pan to be ground into sausage later. We would have tenderloin, bacon, ham, pork chops, ribs, sausage, and headcheese. There was very little of the hog that was not used. Old-timers used to say, "The only part of a hog that can't be used is the squeal."

When the first hog had been cut up, the meat was carried to the springhouse where it would stay cold until it could all be cured, canned, or cooked.

The water was dumped from the tank, the rocks put back in the fire and the tank refilled with hot water from the kettle, and the second hog was hooked to the pulley and manipulated over the tank.

While the men cut up the second hog, Mamma stirred the fat with a long-handled wooden paddle. She kept adding wood to the fire as needed to keep the kettle at the right temperature.

It seemed to take forever for the fat to cook down, leaving crisp chunks called cracklings. When Mamma determined that all the lard had been rendered from the fat, the cracklings were lifted out with a slotted spoon into a large colander that had been placed in one of the crocks, allowing as much fat as possible to drain into the crock.

"Ruth, you must not touch the cracklings until they are cool. You could get a terrible burn," Mamma cautioned. We children could scarcely wait until the cracklings cooled to dip into this delicacy, and Mamma knew it.

The heavy kettle was swung away from the fire. With heavy mitts, George and Papa poured the hot fat from the kettle into five-gallon crocks. This was the lard we would use for baking and frying during the next year. The kettle was swung back over the fire, ready for the fat from the second hog.

Butchering day was a long, hard job, but taking care of the fresh meat was even harder; it took several days.

Papa ground all of the lean trimmings of meat into sausage and seasoned it with his own mixture of spices that included sage and salt mixed with red, white, and black pepper. No one could compete with Papa's sausage.

The hams that were to be smoked were hung in the smokehouse.

Papa used a different combination of seasonings to sugar-cure the hams, shoulders, side meat, and bacon. It included the red, white, and black pepper along with brown sugar and a lot of salt. The process took days. We wrapped the meat in cheesecloth and allowed it to cure in the springhouse.

Mamma formed the sausage into patties and fried them. The cooked patties were placed in the bottom of a crockery jar and the hot fat they were cooked in was poured over them. This was repeated, a layer of sausage covered with a layer of fat, until the jar was nearly full. The top layer was a thick covering of boiling fat. The layers of fat preserved the meat. Mamma covered the jar with a dinner plate and weighted it down with a rock to keep the mice and bugs out. When cool, the jar would be stored in the springhouse. Whenever we wanted sausage, all we had to do was scoop back the top layer of fat, lift out what we needed, place it in a skillet, and heat it. This sausage would last us through the long, cold winter and never spoil.

The bones were all put into a large pot and Mamma boiled them until the meat would fall off. Every scrap of meat was picked from the bones, ground, seasoned, and mixed with some of the broth from the bone pot. Mamma called this headcheese; it tasted like liver sausage.

The meat that wasn't cured, made into headcheese, or ground into sausage had to be used in a few days, or it had to be canned.

Our copper wash boiler was filled about half full of water and set on the cook-stove to boil. A wood lattice-type rack that Papa had made to fit the bottom of the boiler was dropped into the water. Half-gallon blue glass jars were sterilized with boiling water and filled with meat. Mamma put a spoon of salt in each jar, wiped the top with a clean dishcloth, and placed a red rubber ring over the top. When the water in the tub was boiling, she poured boiling water from the teakettle into the jars until it covered the meat. Glass-lined metal jar lids were screwed down tightly against the rubber rings to seal the jars. With a jar lifter, the jars were set into the boiler on the wood rack, leaving space between the jars so the boiling water didn't cause them to hit together and break. If the water didn't cover the jars, more water was added. Mamma knew how long the jars had to boil to cook the meat. When cooked, the jars were lifted out onto a towel and the next batch was placed in the water until all the meat was canned.

This same process was used when we canned chicken or beef. We also used the boiler when we canned fruits and vegetables. We raised, harvested, canned, preserved, or pickled nearly everything we ate.

## Chapter 17

# The Man In The Dark Suit

## 1925

Sometimes, if it became too warm in the kitchen, Mamma would open the door to the parlor. You could feel the cold air rush in when the door was opened. If the parlor was warm, Mamma allowed me to sit on the horsehair sofa and play with the doll she had as a little girl. She was beautiful. Her head, hands, and feet were made of fine porcelain. High-laced shoes were painted on her feet, black wavy hair on her head, and a slight blush on her cheeks. The body was sawdust-filled cloth. Her eyes were a beautiful brown with real eyelashes. When I laid her down, her eyes would close.

"Be careful not to drop your doll. Her head will break easily and it is getting hard to get new porcelain heads for dolls," Mamma cautioned.

Looking out the window, I longed for spring. The leafless trees, revealing empty nests the birds had abandoned when they flew south, looked naked and cold, leaving me with a sad, lonely feeling.

The snow had melted and the ground partially thawed, only to freeze again, leaving footprints and car ruts. It was like a picture of our family's life. Footprints to and from the school bus, mailbox, barnyard, pasture, and back to the house, all sizes and shapes frozen in the mud.

I suddenly became aware of the sound of an automobile approaching. "Mamma, someone is coming."

Mamma came in, drying her hands on her apron. There was a sharp knock on the heavy door as she entered the room. When she opened the door, I saw a man in a dark suit and tie. I knew he wasn't a farmer or one of Papa's customers.

The man handed Mamma some papers. "Mrs. Anderson, I'm sorry I have to serve you with these papers, but it is my job. I want you and Dr. Anderson to know that if there was anything I could do to help, I would. There isn't a farmer in the area that doesn't feel the same. This has always been the Anderson farm. Your husband is just too good. People take advantage of him. Rumor has it that Oscar has skipped out and gone to Texas."

Showing no emotion, Mamma accepted the papers and said, "Thank you Frank. You are right. Hance lives by the Golden Rule. He can't say no to a friend or any one in need. He and Oscar have been friends since childhood. I appreciate your concern. I know our friends would help if they could. With the drought and continued bad crops, every one is having a hard time financially."

"I wish you the best, Mrs. Anderson." With this, he turned and headed for his car. Mamma closed the door and dropped into a chair, buried her face in her apron, and sobbed.

I had never before seen Mamma cry like this and I was frightened. Running to her, I leaned against her quivering body and tried to hug her. "Don't cry," I pleaded. "Why are you crying ?"

Mamma tried to compose herself. Blotting her tears with the corner of her apron, she answered. "They are taking away our home."

"Why Mamma? Why?" I asked.

"I don't think I can explain so you will understand," she said as she tried to compose herself. "Papa's friend Oscar bought new furniture for his house, but he didn't have enough money to pay for it until he harvested his crops. He asked Papa to cosign a note for what he had to borrow. That meant that if Oscar couldn't pay the note, Papa would. Oscar's crops failed and he can't pay the money. Since Papa's crops failed this year, he doesn't have the money either. They will sell this farm to pay Oscar's debt. Your great-great grandfather cleared this land and your grandfather was born on this property. He built this house. Your father, Mabel, Esther, Wayne, and you were all born here."

Mamma was right. I didn't understand. I figured Papa would take care of things when he got home. He always did.

When I was old enough to understand, Mamma told me the story. Papa had a lifelong friend, Oscar, to whom he could never say no. He was a distant cousin of my mother's and never seemed to be able to live within his means. He would borrow money from Papa, and when his crops came in, he would usually pay him back. Oscar bought new furniture for his house, but he didn't have enough money to pay for it until he harvested his crops, so he went to the bank. They wanted more collateral than his crops. When Papa cosigned Oscar's note, he didn't realize he was putting his whole farm up as collateral.

Most people think that the depression started with the stock market crash in 1929. The farmers in the Midwest could tell you differently. Their depression started in the early 1920's with drought and failing crops. There were no laws to control what lenders could do. They could take everything you owned, regardless of value, to cover even a small note.

When Papa came home, he and Mamma went into their bedroom and closed the door. Some time later, the door opened and Papa came out. He had a stern look on his face as he walked across the room to the kitchen door. "I'll tell you one thing, Gladys. They will never get the sheepskin deed." I heard the outside door slam behind him and then the car start.

I was terrified. I felt my whole world was turned upside down. "Mamma, where is Papa going?"

"He is going to talk to Aunt Mae and the boys.

"Why don't you run get your coat and you can take Esther down to the end of the lane to watch for the school bus while I start supper." Reluctantly, I did as I was told.

When Papa returned home, he told Mamma, "I have told Floyd and George to come take anything they can use that we won't be able to take with us. I think they will take the horses and mules until I can sell the ones they don't want to keep. The cows, sheep, and hogs I can put with some of my clients. They will be glad to keep them on shares."

I would learn later that this meant we would get half of the newborn animals and half of the meat at butchering time.

The next night, and for several nights later, I heard trucks and wagons pulling in and out of our yard. I heard the bellowing of cows, the bleating of sheep, and the grunting, snorting sound of hogs as they were loaded and hauled away.

For days, Mamma and Tracy packed boxes in between cooking, laundry, answering the constantly ringing phone, and taking care of children. Mamma would ask me to watch Esther and entertain Wayne while she worked. Boxes were carried out into the yard and packed into trucks and wagons. Mamma said they were going to our new home. It was like spring cleaning. All the rugs were rolled up. The rooms were almost empty except for our beds. After supper, we were sent off to bed while the moving continued. The noise of the moving didn't keep me awake.

I didn't even awaken when Papa carried me to the car. Our beds were taken apart and packed into the truck. The truck was sent on ahead with Raymond and Arthur. Papa, Mamma, Mabel, Esther, Wayne and I went in the car.

I awakened in a strange room. Esther was sleeping next to me. I recognized my bed. Slipping out of it, I ran down the stairs, relieved to see Mamma fixing breakfast.

I wandered through the house between packing boxes and furniture and out onto the porch. The house sat on a high hill with a view of the Tippecanoe River in the distance. There were no woods or huge fields of grain. I could hear the roosters crowing and the screeching of the guinea hens. This made me feel better. Everything was strange. We had left 240 acres and now lived on 12 acres. Papa wouldn't call it a farm. He said it was nothing but a truck patch. I found he had brought 2 of our cows, 2 sows, all of our chickens, ducks, guinea hens, and geese. Papa must have worked most of the night moving, and had left early this morning on calls.

House on the hill, summer and winter

Our new home was exciting for a few days. It was like an adventure. I hadn't realized that we were staying here permanently. I wanted to go home to the farm. Mamma had tried to explain, but it didn't make sense to a five-year-old. My life would never be the same.

Now Mamma seldom sang as she worked. She would become cross over little things. Papa seemed tired and sad. He worked longer and longer hours and brought home less money. Many times he would bring home a side of beef, a ham, or a bag of beans as payment on a bill.

I would learn later that Oscar, after the statute of limitations ran out, returned to the area with his family and started farming again. When his animals became sick, he would call my father and Papa would go, day or night. He might spend the night treating a cow with milk fever or delivering a calf.

Mamma would complain, "Hance, why do you go? You know you won't get paid. He cost us our farm."

"Gladys, when I became a vet, I took an oath. If I refused to go, who would I be hurting? Oscar's wife and children would suffer. The animals might die. Neither his wife nor his animals did anything to me. Don't you understand? It is my Christian duty and my obligation as a veterinarian to take care of his animals."

Mamma would shake her head. She knew he would never go against his Christian beliefs.

To this day, my heart aches when I think of that farm and the wonderful memories of the life I knew there. I have often wondered what happened to the sheepskin deed. Did Papa give it to George or Floyd? I am sure the bank didn't get it.

# Chapter 18

*Unsettled On The Hill*

Our first Sunday in our new home, Mamma got us dressed in our Sunday clothes and gave us each a penny to put in the collection plate. Raymond was given orders to see that we got to Sunday school and home safely.

It was a mile to town and the Presbyterian Church. Raymond, Arthur, Mabel, and I ran down what seemed like 100 steps, (I counted them years later; there were thirty) to the gravel road in front of the house, and headed for church. We had gone about halfway when we came to the bridge over the Tippecanoe. The roadbed of the bridge had been paved over, but the pedestrian walkway was made of wood planks with small cracks between to allow water to drain off. That would have been fine, but I did not know how to swim and I was terrified of falling in. I started across. As I looked down, those cracks seemed to grow bigger and bigger. There were planks missing in some areas. The City didn't have the money to replace them. When I came to a spot where a board was missing, I froze.

Raymond, who had been fussing at me because I was

going to make him late, grabbed my hand and literally ran, making me follow. When we finally got to the church, we were assigned to classes according to our age.

My teacher was Miss Burns. She also taught the first grade where I was to attend next fall.

I loved Sunday school and my teacher, but I dreaded the trip home over that bridge. I began to plan how I could get across without Raymond's help. When we got near the bridge, I took off running as fast as I could, over the paved area of the bridge. Fortunately, there were no cars coming. I was able to avoid Raymond's help after that.

We had moved to the hill shortly before Easter. Monticello, a small city with a population of approximately 3000, had more and larger stores in which Mamma could shop. Grandpa lived in town now, and Mamma was happy to be near Grandpa Arrick and her sister Winona. Grandpa was delighted to have his beloved daughter so close.

One morning, Grandpa arrived in his old Ford. Mamma left us with our new hired girl, Beatrice Westerhouse, and went to town with him. When she returned, she had two large hatboxes. From one box she removed a stack of three identical hats. She had bought each of us girls a new Easter hat. They were black straw with a wide brim and a long black satin ribbon that wrapped around the crown, tied in a bow at the back, and fell down below our shoulders. In the other box was the most beautiful royal blue velvet hat I had ever seen.

When Papa came home, Mamma hurried to model her new hat for him. "I bought new Easter hats for the girls also," she announced.

"Gladys, how much did you spend?"

Mamma could see Papa was not pleased. "I got all four

hats for $16.00. The girls need hats for church." Mamma had never before had to watch what she spent.

Papa had been on calls all day and was tired and dirty. "Gladys! We have just lost our home. How could you spend sixteen dollars for hats when we don't know where our next meal is coming from?"

I had never before heard Papa angry at anything Mamma did. Sixteen dollars didn't mean anything to me, but Papa's statement sank in. Suddenly I realized we were poor. Did Papa mean maybe we wouldn't have food to eat? I knew we had jars of sausage that Mamma had cooked and stored. We had canned beef, chicken, fruit and vegetables that Mamma had canned. We still had smoked hams and bacon. We had two cows and our chickens. I didn't understand.

I took my new hat upstairs and placed it on the dresser where it would be safe until Easter Sunday.

Even though we had been living in our new home for almost a month, we still weren't completely moved in. You can't move three generations of possessions on a weekend.

Because church and school (in that order) came first in our family, Papa made arrangements for wagons to move us on Saturdays, when the boys were home to help. Papa had brought as much as he could in his old car each time he was on calls in that area. Each Saturday, he, Mamma and the boys left early and returned after dark.

Before anything was put away, Mamma and Beatrice scrubbed windows, shelves, woodwork and floors. The carpets we had brought with us had been hung over the clotheslines and beaten with a carpet beater to remove any dust or sand. They were then rolled and placed at one end of the room in which they would be laid.

The center of the wood floor, where the carpet would go, was bare wood. The floor beyond this was varnished. Strips from a large roll of heavy red colored paper were cut to fit the bare wood. This was to protect the back of the carpet from wear. The rolled carpet was placed at one end of the paper and unrolled.

Gradually things were put in place, but boxes never seemed to disappear. When one bunch was emptied, another stack took its place.

A long narrow room, off the dining room, became Papa's medicine room. We all understood that room was off limits. The dining room was large enough to hold our table opened to seat fourteen people and still have room for cupboards along the wall. A door on the north wall opened onto a covered porch.

A wide archway with folding doors (that were never closed) separated the dining room from the living room. You could step out onto a small porch on the north side of the dining room. The living room was a large square room with south and west windows. Our living room door opened onto a covered porch that went across the front of the house, wrapping around the corner through a breezeway in front of the kitchen door, to the pump and the backyard. Wisteria grew on a trellis across the front of the porch. From our front porch we had a magnificent view down our hill, across the road to the Tippecanoe River as well as the woods and homes that bordered it. We could see the comings and goings from Trig Randal's bootleg joint on the water.

In the northeast corner of the living room was the door to the upstairs bedrooms. You climbed up about 6 or 8 steps to a landing and another 4 steps to the boy's bedroom. We had to go through the boys' room to get to the girls' room. Both rooms were large enough to hold two full beds. There were windows on the east and south walls of the boys' room and the south and west walls in the girls' room, allowing for good ventilation and a view of the river and Dutch Roth's home at the bottom of the hill.

Mamma's and Papa's room was just below the boys' room and could be entered from the living room or the kitchen. There was a toilet in a small room in the corner of this bedroom, which no one was allowed to use. Papa had discovered it did not empty into a cesspool but had been piped under the garden about three hundred feet beyond the house and emptied out on the side of the hill. We all used the outhouse.

You could enter the kitchen from Mamma's bedroom, the dining room, or the porch. Under a window in the southeast corner of the kitchen was a large sink mounted to the wall. Next to it was a counter for the washbasin and a small, red, cast-iron pump that pumped rainwater from the cistern.

To the left of the sink was a door leading to a covered area between the house and the smokehouse. On the northeast wall stood our old cook stove with the wood-box behind it. To the left of the stove was a door into a large walk-in pantry. In the middle of the west wall was Mamma's kitchen cabinet and a work counter where a three-gallon bucket full of water always stood. To the left was the door to the dining room. In the middle of the kitchen stood a drop-leaf table where Mamma made bread, pies, and cookies, and prepared meals.

We girls delighted ourselves running a complete circle through the house until Mamma would raise her voice and say, "That's enough. If you girls want to play, go outside."

Our new home was still a mile from town, but we now had electric lights and a phone that you didn't have to crank, and we could call anyplace. You lifted the black cone-shaped receiver from its cradle on the side of the phone and placed it to your ear. A pleasant voice would say, "Number please." Our number was 477 and it was a private line. I'll bet the party lines missed Mamma. There were a lot of lonely farm wives who used the phone for entertainment and to keep up with their neighbors' well-being.

Papa's territory was in different phone districts. Now, to call another district, Mamma asked the operator to connect her to the operator of that phone company, and that operator would make the connection to the party she was calling.

It was Saturday, a beautiful, sunny, spring day. Papa, Mamma and the boys had left at daybreak to go back to the farm for the final load of furniture and boxes, the things we were unable to bring when we first moved into the house on the hill. Beatrice had been left in charge of us three girls. We called her "Bea." Esther and I were standing in our bare living room, watching Beatrice as she sat curling Mabel's hair. Suddenly she laid down the comb, saying, "I smell smoke," as she dashed out onto the porch and around the house. She was only gone seconds when she dashed back into the house shouting, "The house is on fire! You girls get out into the yard! I have to call the fire department and then I will come out with you."

Mabel grabbed Esther's hand and immediately obeyed. The only thing I could think of was my new Easter hat. I didn't want it to burn. I was sure I would never get another one. I dashed up the stairs, grabbed the beautiful black straw hat and was in the yard before Bea knew I was missing.

Firemen had placed ladders against the house and were working on the roof over the kitchen. Water was being pumped up to them from their fire truck and sprayed onto the roof. They determined that a spark from the chimney of the kitchen stove had ignited the roof of the smokehouse. It was quickly put out and fortunately there was no damage to the house or its contents.

I dashed back up the stairs with my hat, excited that I would have a story to tell Papa when he got home. Bea was our hero.

Easter Sunday, we all got dressed in our Sunday clothes. Raymond and Arthur, dressed up in their suits with the knee-high breeches, starched white shirts and ties had decided to walk rather than have to hold a sister on their lap (our family had outgrown our car). Papa loaded the rest of us in the car and headed for town. We three girls wore our new hats and Mamma wore her beautiful blue velvet hat with a dress that matched. Papa looked so handsome in his suit, starched white shirt, and tie. He hated getting dressed up, but he did it to please Mamma. Papa wasn't comfortable in the Presbyterian Church. He considered it too liberal and that too many people went to show off their fine clothes rather than to hear the Gospel; however, since there wasn't a Seceder Church nearby, it was important that his children attend a church that did not stray from God's Word.

# Chapter 19

# Dr. Krey and His Black Bag

## June 1, 1925

Papa awakened me and said, "All your sisters and brothers are out in the orchard, and I want you to go out with them until Bea calls you to breakfast." He helped me dress. I was still half asleep, but I followed him down the stairs.

As we stepped into the living room, I saw a strange man sleeping in Papa's chair, with his feet up on Papa's roll-top desk. There was a black bag sitting on the floor beside him. I looked up at Papa, but he held a finger to his lips and hurried me outside.

"That man is Dr. Krey. He is here to see Mamma. You run play with your sisters and brothers. We will call you when breakfast is ready."

When I reached the orchard, Mabel rushed and announced that I didn't get to see Raymond kill a snake. Now my day was ruined. Why didn't they wake me earlier?

Raymond was trying to get Arthur to bet on whether

Mamma was going to have one baby or two. "I'll bet it is twins. What do you bet?" Arthur wouldn't bet.

How did they know she was going to have a baby? Then I remembered the strange man with the black bag. It couldn't be twins, I reasoned. That bag isn't big enough for two babies. I am glad I didn't think out loud. Raymond would have held that over my head for the rest of my life.

Finally I heard Bea calling from the back door, "You can come in now. Breakfast is ready."

When we walked in, the strange man was gone. We went into Mamma's bedroom. Papa was sitting on the edge of their bed, smiling, with a tiny baby in the palm of each hand. Mamma smiled as she watched each of us greet our new sisters.

We all gathered around Papa. He held the babies where I could touch their tiny fingers. They were like tiny identical dolls. As I looked at them I thought, "Maybe, as tiny as they are, they could fit in that black bag."

Papa said, "One weighs five pounds and the other five and one-half. They are identical twins. We have tied different colored ribbons around their wrists so we won't get them mixed up.

Mamma and Papa had agreed on names for the twins. The firstborn, the largest, was named Mary Helen Agnes, and her twin was Margaret Ellen Ida. The third name was to honor their grandmothers whom they had never known, Agnes after Grandma Anderson and Ida after Grandma Arrick.

It seemed that every day one or more of our friends and relatives came to see the twins. Our babies became cuter by the day. When they were first born, we couldn't tell them apart, so we just called them Twinnie when we talked to them. As they grew, if you looked closely, Mary's face was a little fuller than Margaret's, but you had to look directly into their faces to recognize them. Most people could not tell them apart. As a result, they were called Twinnie most of the time. This came in handy when they were in high school. One was better at one subject, the other better at another, so they would switch classes to cover for each other. They knew which teachers couldn't tell them apart.

Life changed with two new babies and a very active 22-month-old boy. Mamma would remind me that I would be six in November and I was old enough to help. Wayne was a full-time job and he became my responsibility. I didn't mind. I loved my little brother, but sometimes he was more than I could handle.

*Chapter 20*

# My First Day Of School

## September 1925

All summer I had been looking forward to school. In late August, Mamma took me shopping for new shoes. I had never before had shoes with laces. My shoes had always had buttons. I had to use a button hook to button them. Papa showed me how to tie my new shoes and sat with me while I practiced tying them myself.

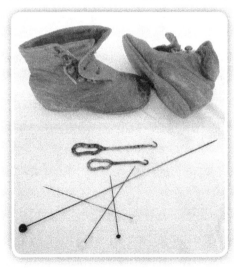

I begged Mamma to cut my hair. She lifted a curl and said, "Papa says, a woman's hair is her Crown In Glory."

Ruth's high-button shoes with shoe hooks, and Mamma's hat pins

I thought to myself, "I wonder if God would mind if my crown was short?"

I had made friends with a neighbor girl, Merdith Fowler. We were going to attend the South Side School together. This school only had two grades, first and second. Miss Burns was to be my teacher.

The week before school started, Mamma took me in to Boyd's barbershop to have my hair cut. Tears welled up in her eyes as she watched him cut. Mr. Boyd said, "I will save you some of her curls, Mrs. Anderson."

On the first day of school, Mamma called up the stairs, "Breakfast is ready. Hurry and get dressed so you don't miss the bus. I was the first one up and dressed in my new hand-me-down dress from Mabel, my long cotton stockings with elastic garters and my string-tied shoes. I could comb my own short hair. When the bus came, I ran down the steps with my brothers and Mabel. I was so excited. This was the day I had looked forward to all summer.

Miss Burns was standing at the door, greeting us as we entered the building. We were assigned seats in alphabetical order. Everything was wonderful. When recess time came, we filed out onto the playground and ran for swings, the maypole or the monkey bars.

I was swinging on the maypole when Miss Burns called me in. She said, "Ruth, this is Mr. Elder. Mr. Elder is the Principal of the school. He wants to talk to you."

Mr. Elder leaned over and said, "Ruth, we are going to take a little ride up to see another school."

Shaking my head, I looked from Mr. Elder to Miss Burns. "It is all right, Ruth. Your mother knows."

Mr. Elder said, "Bring your dinner bucket and come with me."

"Can I come back?" I asked.

"Yes," he answered.

I followed Mr. Elder to his car, got in, and sat as far from him as I could. When we got to the Lincoln building, he took me into a classroom, introduced me to Miss Prevo, and left. I looked around and saw no one that I knew.

Miss Prevo greeted me and said, "Ruth, you go put your dinner pail in the cloak room. When you come back, you may sit in this seat," pointing to a desk in the front of the room. I did as I was told.

Miss Prevo passed out papers and said we were going to learn penmanship. She had drawn lines on the blackboard. Picking up a piece of chalk, she proceeded to draw circles on top of circles, like a tight spring, all across the paper. "Keep your circles between the lines and fill the full page," she said. As we worked, she walked between the rows of seats, checking to see that we were holding our pencils correctly and observing our work.

When the lunch bell rang, Miss Prevo said, "That is the lunch bell, children. You may put your work in your desks. The first row will line up and file into the cloak room, get your lunch pails, and bring them back to your desks. I will let you know when the other rows may follow."

I was in the first row and did as she said. When I returned to the room, instead of sitting down, I headed for the door. Miss Prevo grabbed my arm and jerked me back. "Ruth Anderson, where do you think you are going?"

I looked up into her angry face. I was terrified. In a shaking voice I answered, "I am going back to the Southside School. Mr. Elder promised me I could go back there."

Angrily, she swung me around and threw me into my seat as she said in a loud angry voice, "You aren't going anyplace. You were transferred to this class and this is where you are going to stay. Now eat your lunch, and I don't want any more trouble with you."

Mr. Elder had lied to me. I didn't know that grownups lied to children. I didn't like this school or Miss Prevo. She was mean and had embarrassed me in front of the whole class. I didn't know anyone and I didn't want to be here. Miss Burns and all my friends were at the Southside School. I was too upset to eat my lunch. All my excitement about going to school had been jerked out of me.

I managed to get through the day and joined Mabel and my brothers on the school bus. When I got home, I ran up the steps looking for Mamma. I thought she would call and get me back in Miss Burns class. By this time, all the tears I had been holding back were flowing. I sobbed out my story, but when I said Mr. Elder had lied and I hated Miss Prevo, she stopped me.

"Now Ruth, I am sure you must have misunderstood Mr. Elder. I don't believe he would lie to you. Miss Burns called me and said her class was too big and the Principal had informed her that one child had to be transferred. To be fair, they went in alphabetical order. "A" is the first letter in the alphabet and Anderson begins with "A." You must never say you hate anyone. This is Miss Prevo's first year as a teacher; you must give her a chance. I know her mother and father, and they are very nice people."

It was a hard lesson, but I learned that the teacher was always right and it did no good to tell Mamma when they weren't.

I cried when I was forced to go to school the next morning. School was a nightmare. I was too afraid to recite, answer questions, or ask for help if I needed it. I figured it wouldn't do any good to tell Mamma, so I withdrew into myself. Since most of the other children had gone to kindergarten together and had made their friends, I was ignored. (Papa said kindergarten was for people who didn't want to take care of their own children, so we didn't go.)

The only bright spot in my first year of school was a little girl named Florence Irons. She came up to me one day, took my hand and said, "You are going to be my friend." She was right. We became very close friends. We were inseparable until, at the end of the year, when her father moved their family to a farm in nearby Chalmers. She would be going to school there. Even after she moved, we wrote to each other for years, but I never saw her again.

## Chapter 21

# The Black Plush Coat

By 1926, although the stock market was skyrocketing, many farmers had lost their farms. This was due to drought, failing crops, and poor business decisions. My father was no exception. When we lost our farm in early 1925, our family consisted of my parents and six children: Raymond age 11, Arthur 9½, Mabel 7, Ruth 5, Esther 3, and Wayne 1½. Now, with the twins, there were eight of us. Our father, being a veterinarian, was dependent upon the farmers for his income.

It was late November. The rosy glow of red-hot coals showing through the icing-glass windows of our huge baseburner sent cozy warmth throughout our living room. I was sitting on the floor, stacking blocks for Wayne, who was three and a very happy child. The minute I got the blocks stacked, he would knock them down and shout with laughter.

Papa was sitting at his roll-top desk, logging calls. Mamma, in her rocker nearby, was darning stockings. Although they spoke in hushed tones, I heard every word. They had no idea that I worried with them. I heard Mamma say, "Hance, what are we going to do? The children need new winter clothes

"Gladys, I don't know what more I can do."

"Can't you go to some of the farmers who owe you money and try to collect? You are carrying so many of them on the books. Ruth is wearing a coat that was handed down from Mabel, and she has worn it for two years. It's threadbare. If we could get Mabel a new coat, Ruth could wear Mabel's old one for a couple of years."

"I will try, Gladys, but if the farmers had money, I am sure they would pay me. I can't ask them to pay me and have their families go hungry. At least our children never go to bed hungry. Keep sending out the bills. When I make calls, I will try to get them to pay something on their back bills. We just have to have faith. God has provided for us so far."

Until we lost our farm, we wanted for nothing. Suddenly, we were poor. I was in the first grade and very conscious of my worn hand-me-downs when I saw other girls in nice, new, warm coats.

At recess, I managed to be the last out of the cloakroom and onto the playground. Instead of joining in the games, I ran to a stairwell leading to a classroom, partially below ground. The steps went down about four feet. Hiding in the stairwell, I was protected from the cold winter wind and no one could see me. When the bell rang, I dashed in, took off the hated coat, and hung it over my lunch pail.

Each night, our entire family gathered around Papa as he read from the Bible. When he finished, everyone knelt beside their chair with hands folded as Papa prayed. We all knew that this was a time of reverence, and no one made a sound, not even Raymond. After prayer, Mamma and Papa kissed us goodnight. "Don't forget to say your prayers," Mamma called after us.

Rushing up the stairs, I quickly changed into my flannel gown and crawled under the heavy covers of the bed I shared with my sister Esther.

The Bible verse Papa had read was running through my mind. Jesus said if I asked for anything in His name, I would get it. So I prayed, "Lord, I really need a new coat and Papa can't afford it because he can't make the children go to bed hungry. Maybe you could give the farmers money so they can pay Papa. Then he could buy me a coat. If you can't make money for the farmers, maybe you could find a coat someplace and give it to me. Papa read from the Bible and it said that if I ask anything in Jesus' name I would receive it. So I'm asking You in Jesus' name. Please bring me a coat."

Every night I prayed this prayer and each day expected a coat to appear. When it didn't, I figured God was just too busy. It was almost Christmas and He must be having lots of requests. But I didn't give up. I kept praying, thinking that maybe He would hear me.

The last day of school before Christmas vacation, I went into the cloakroom. There on a hanger was the most beautiful black plush coat I had ever seen. Hanging my tattered coat on a hook, I started to put my dinner bucket under it. I looked longingly at the black coat. There was no dinner bucket under it, so I slid mine over and pretended it was mine. Near the end of the day, the teacher said, "Ruth Anderson, wait after school. I want to see you."

I was terrified. What had I done? When the classroom was cleared, Miss Prevo led me into the cloakroom. I was shaking so hard, I could scarcely walk. I thought I must have done something awful and was going to be punished. Maybe it was because I put my dinner bucket under that coat.

Lifting the beautiful coat from the hanger, she turned to me and said, "Let's see if this fits you." In disbelief, I tried it on. It was so soft and warm. I kept running my hands over the fur-like material.

My eyes must have been as big as saucers as I looked up at my teacher and asked, "Whose coat is this?"

"It is yours. Miss Orton made it for you." Miss Orton was Mabel's Sunday school teacher.

"May I take it home?"

"Of course. It's yours. There is a note in the pocket and some extra buttons. Be careful not to lose them. Run along now or you will miss your bus."

Bursting with pride and joy, I climbed onto the bus. Then a horrible thought struck me. What if Mamma won't let me keep it? Maybe she will think it is Charity, and we don't take Charity. I had heard her say that.

The bus stopped at the foot of our hill. As I climbed the steps up the steep hill to the house, I tried to think of arguments if Mamma said no. When I reached the front door, it opened and Mamma smiled down at me. "Do you like your new coat?" she asked.

"Yes, Mamma. Miss Orton made it for me." I was jumping with joy as I turned to show her the beautiful coat.

"I know. She called me and asked if she could. She made it from one of her old coats. You must be sure to thank her when you go to Sunday school. Papa is in the front room. Run and show him."

"Papa! Papa! See my new coat! Miss Orton made it for

me. I was waiting for God to bring me one. I prayed every night for a new coat and I prayed in Jesus' name, like you read from the Bible. I guess God was too busy to get around to it, but now He doesn't need to. I have one."

Papa gathered me onto his lap and gave me a big hug. Pulling a handkerchief from his pocket, he blew his nose and dabbed at his eyes. "Purtsy, God is never too busy to answer prayers. We just never know how or when He will do it. God has thousands of helpers that he calls upon to help him answer prayers. This time He spoke to Miss Orton and said, 'DON'T THROW THAT OLD COAT AWAY. Look for someone who can use it.' Miss Orton saw you in a worn out coat and she knew you were the one. See Ruth, God answered your prayers. Remember this, Ruth, when you do a kind deed for someone, you may be helping God answer someone's prayer."

I have never forgotten the lessons I learned at Papa's knee.

# About the Author

Winona Ruth Gunther, the fourth of twelve children, writes of her childhood memories in "Papa Said." While raising two children, Ruth hosted a radio interview program and later became a Realtor. Retired, she lives in the home she shared with her late husband in Solana Beach, California, overlooking the Pacific Ocean.

CPSIA information can be obtained
at www.ICGtesting.com
Printed in the USA
LVHW110101080220
646300LV00001B/137